W9-CBH-982

Ready
for
Preschool

PREPARE YOUR CHILD FOR HAPPINESS
AND SUCCESS AT SCHOOL

Ready *for* Preschool

PRUFROCK PRESS INC.
WACO, TEXAS

Nancy B. Hertzog, Ph.D.

Library of Congress Cataloging-in-Publication Data

Hertzog, Nancy B., 1955–
  Ready for preschool : prepare your child for happiness and success at school / Nancy B.
Hertzog.
     p. cm.
  Includes bibliographical references.
  ISBN-13: 978-1-59363-311-0 (pbk.)
  ISBN-10: 1-59363-311-4 (pbk.)
  1. Preschool children. 2. Readiness for school. 3. Child development. I. Title.
  HQ774.5.H476 2008
  649'.68—dc22
                         2008013952

Copyright © 2008 Prufrock Press Inc.
Edited by Lacy Elwood
Cover and Layout Design by Marjorie Parker

ISBN-13: 978-1-59363-311-0
ISBN-10: 1-59363-311-4

Printed in the United States of America.

At the time of this book's publication, all facts and figures cited are the most current available.
All telephone numbers, addresses, and Web site URLs are accurate and active. All publications, organizations, Web sites, and other resources exist as described in the book, and all
have been verified. The authors and Prufrock Press Inc. make no warranty or guarantee concerning the information and materials given out by organizations or content found at Web
sites, and we are not responsible for any changes that occur after this book's publication. If
you find an error, please contact Prufrock Press Inc.

Prufrock Press Inc.
P.O. Box 8813
Waco, TX 76714-8813
Phone: (800) 998-2208
Fax: (800) 240-0333
http://www.prufrock.com

Dedication

This book is dedicated to the two boys who taught me about parenting, Jacob Bruce and Brian James, and my parenting partner David. At different times, both boys questioned how I could be such a patient teacher of other people's children, but so impatient with them at home. How true that is! I had all kinds of advice that I garnered from my educational repertoire, but often had difficulty following it for my own children. When talking with parents of preschoolers, I learned to preface it by saying, "the research shows such and such . . ." or "it worked for my family, but . . ." I never assume it will work for the family that I am talking to. I appreciate now more than ever the role of the experimentalist, and the influence that my husband as an experimental physicist has had on me. My children have taught me how precious each stage of child development really is—get into their moments. Enjoy their early years, their elementary school age years, their teen years, and yes, even try to embrace their first loves! My sons' interests—rock music, jazz, soccer, acting, skateboarding, gaming, and the newest technologies—have enriched my life immeasurably. I am ever so grateful to have such a family!

Contents

Introduction

I enjoyed planning my personal and professional life—when to go to graduate school, when to get married, when to have children. My first child was scheduled to come at the end of the school year so that I could finish all of my teaching responsibilities and take off the summer months, never really needing a maternity leave. Instead, he came 2 months early while I was attending a Junior Great Books Conference! My whopping 2 ½ pound baby, now 21, became a jazz guitarist. Who would have thought that his intense interests in dinosaurs, tools, airplanes, and guitars would have culminated into a career as a jazz musician? And, having no musical ability whatsoever, how can I continually support (not monetarily, I hope) his professional pursuits?

Those 21 years have been filled with surprises (and much less faith in my own planning ability). Now with two sons becoming young adults, what continually amazes me is how much I do not know about parenting, even though I should know (professionally) about children. I continue to ask myself, "What can and what can't I do as a parent?" The answers to these questions change as children go through different stages of their lives. I found out the hard way never to volunteer to chaperone for a dance in middle school and never assume that a child with a car will come "straight" home from school.

For many of you, the first few years of your child's school life are milestones in your lives, as well. You are experiencing early successes in your career, negotiating your children with different sets of grandparents, and trying to strike a balance between work and home, all of the time wanting to do what's best for your children. You are asking yourselves, "What can I do to support my child's growth and learning?" and "What can I do to get my child ready for school?" You also are realizing there are things that you cannot do. You cannot make a child learn, or make him have friends. You can provide the supporting and nurturing home environment that fosters the love of learning, that encourages risk taking, and builds self-esteem and self-confidence. Some of the things that contribute to this nurturing environment are easier than others to achieve.

As parents you are making thousands of decisions each day. You are deciding what your children are allowed to watch on television, what foods they will eat, what friends you will encourage your child to bring to your home, what extracurricular activities are valued (e.g., sports, religious or community events), how much time the child can spend in front of a computer, and how you will spend time with your children. Most of the time you're making decisions on the spot while you are at the checkout counter in the grocery store, when you pick up your children at daycare and they ask to go to someone's house, when they talk you into reading the fifth book before bed, and so on. You have control of many of the decisions about your children when they are young. But your aim is not to maintain control. Your goal is to empower your children to make their own decisions. They too will decide what they will watch on television, what they will eat, and with whom they will play when parents are not around. You want to make sure that when they are making their own decisions, they will have the competencies and the value systems to choose wisely.

Why Read This Book?

The sense of a need for school readiness has always loomed over parents. But with new No Child Left Behind (2001) emphases on ensuring every child read proficiently by third grade, the urge of greater literacy and school readiness among young children has grown. In a recent *Newsweek* article, "The New First Grade: Too Much Too Soon," several kindergarten programs were explored to point to the rising stakes of early education—more children are coming to kindergarten to do more than finger-paint or learn their letters and numbers; for many, kindergarten means the start of reading instruction (Tyre, 2006). For some kids, the article notes, reading abilities are already in place when the child starts kindergarten. This isn't to say that you should run out and enroll your 3-year-old in a reading tutorial program, but to note that school readiness—and more than just literacy readiness, physical and social readiness, as well—is an important concern. As a parent, you're not alone in wanting to ensure your child is ready for schooling, including preschool.

The purpose of this book is to help guide you in making some of those decisions that will positively impact the growth and well-being of your child before he or she ever steps foot in a classroom. The chapters focus on things parents can do and decisions parents can make to increase their children's competencies in social and physical, as well as academic domains. We'll focus mostly on recognizing readiness in children and developing readiness through everyday activities and situations. (Despite what marketing companies would have you believe, Baby Einstein DVDs and fancy tutoring programs are not necessary to develop a child's cognitive skills. Simple errands and around-the-house tasks often do the job just as well, and with more fun for child and parent.) This book also will strive to provide you with the means of making those important decisions about what schools to choose and how to make the transition from time with mom (or dad) to time with teacher.

Overview of the Chapters

In Chapter 1, the concept of school readiness is discussed within the context of both research and policies. The relationship of the child to the school environment will be explored in depth. In addition, information on the signs of physical and academic readiness, as well as a basic overview of the skill sets most preschool-age children should develop before entering a school setting, will be discussed.

Chapter 2 will focus on practical strategies parents can do to provide a home environment that encourages the growth of specific social and academic skills. This chapter will have a number of activities that parents can do at home to get their children "ready" for school and will include a variety of ways parents can adapt situations outside the home into learning opportunities.

Behavior problems often are cited as a major barrier to success in the early school years. Chapter 3 will discuss the relationship between behavior and social and emotional competencies. Resources to enhance a child's emotional growth will be provided, including a detailed list of books appropriate for addressing emotions with preschool-age children.

Chapter 4 will include a discussion of the types of preschool programs and environments that are most compatible for the growth and well-being of the child. In particular, this chapter gives specific examples of different types of curricular models that parents may see when they enter early childhood classrooms and guidance to parents looking to make the decision about which school environment will be right for their child.

Chapter 5 gives practical suggestions for strengthening partnerships between school and home. Many examples of how parents can become involved in their child's education will be discussed.

Chapter 6 gives parents tips for "letting go" of their youngsters. Attention to how parents help children make transitions and how to ease the transition from home to school for the parents will be included.

Chapter 7 summarizes the accumulated strategies in the book and gives parents guidance for pursuing answers to their specific questions by accessing resources from publications and professional organizations. An extensive list of resources is included at the back of this book.

All children are eager and ready for school; perhaps this book will help you be ready for your child's school too!

Chapter 1

Ready to Learn or Ready for School?

Getting Ready vs. Readiness

All children in America will start school ready to learn. (Goals 2000 Educate America Act, 1994)

IN 1994, to prepare for the next century, President Clinton and the nation's state governors convened for an education conference that resulted in the Goals 2000 Educate America Act, later passed into legislation by the 103rd Congress. The first goal, "All children in America will start school ready to learn," renewed emphasis on the importance the impact of early childhood environments have on future learning potential. The National School Readiness Task Force issued a report meant to encourage and guide public policy and community efforts to achieve this first goal. The report included a redefinition of school readiness. Excerpts of that definition follow:

- School readiness involves not only academic knowledge and skills, but also physical health, self-confidence, and social competence.

- School readiness is not determined solely by the abilities and capacities of young children. It is shaped and developed by people and environments.
- School readiness is not determined solely by the quality of early childhood programs. Readiness also depends on the expectations and capacities of teachers and elementary schools.
- School readiness also is the responsibility of communities, because they have a stake in and an obligation to support families in the development of healthy young children (National Association of State Boards of Education, 1991).

Thirteen years later, school readiness is now more than ever a hot topic in both public policy forums and educational practice. New state initiatives such as Illinois' Preschool for All prioritize funding for programs where the majority of children ages 3 to 4 come from homes that have risk factors (Illinois State Board of Education, 2008; ISBE). Such risk factors may include children from high poverty levels, those with a single parent, those who speak English as a second language, and those with a developmental delay or a specific disability. A major goal of the Preschool for All initiative is to provide higher qualified personnel to children who are in home or center daycare environments than are currently being provided (ISBE, 2008). Preschool for All teachers must be state certified in early childhood education. Thus, Preschool for All teachers may teach in home daycare, private daycare centers, or in public preschool programs as long as 2 ½ hours per day of instruction at these centers is considered preschool (ISBE, 2008). The Preschool for All initiative theoretically broadens the types of settings and environments to provide quality early childhood education in an effort to jumpstart the academic and social readiness skills that are required for most kindergartens.

Another initiative by the same name is the Preschool for All program developed by the Collaborative for Children and the Center for Houston's Future. Working in Houston, TX, these organizations have come together to bring quality preschool education to all 3- and 4-year-old students in the greater Houston area. The groups' efforts include integrating the current education and childcare options (public prekindergarten, Head Start, and licensed daycare) to allow the three systems of education to provide:

- quality cognitive foundations for school readiness and success,
- a safe and loving environment where trusting relationships can be fostered and healthy social/emotional foundations can be created,
- a consistent setting in one facility with hours to accommodate the parent, and
- quality professional development for understanding how young children learn. (Preschool for All, n.d., ¶ 6)

Early intervention programs are based on the premise that there are specific skills and competencies children need to have before they come to school to be more successful in school. But, the focus on readiness also has had a negative impact. Many districts have policies that encourage parents to delay placing their child in kindergarten or even worse, create classrooms of children who are not yet "ready" for kindergarten. Leaders in the field of early childhood education do not support the notion that if children do not have readiness skills by the time they turn kindergarten age (which is an arbitrary date across the 50

.S.), they should be placed in separate classes or
1 entering kindergarten.

1al Association for the Education of Young Children
2ves "it is the responsibility of schools to meet the
needs of children as they enter school and to provide whatever
services are needed to help each child reach his or her fullest
potential" (2004, p. 1). Readiness no longer is seen as a responsibility of families. Community agencies, states, and the federal
government are contributing programs that presumably provide
more resources for children to improve their capacity to be successful in school.

School readiness is *broadly defined* by the experts (including
the National Education Goals Panel and the School Readiness
Indicators Initiative) and includes ready children, ready families,
ready communities, ready early care and education, and ready
schools. Referred to as the "ready childhood equation," four components influence children's ability to be ready for school. They
include:

- *Ready Families:* Describes the children's family context
  and home environment.
- *Ready Communities:* Describes the community resources
  and supports available to families with young children.
- *Ready Services:* Describes the availability, quality, and
  affordability of proven programs that influence child
  development and school readiness.
- *Ready Schools:* Describes elements of schools that influence child development and school success. (National
  School Readiness Indicators Initiative, 2005)

This broad definition acknowledges that the reasons all children are not "ready" are bigger than not possessing the prereq-

uisite skills to do well in school. Achievement data show marked differences between outcomes of children from homes in poverty compared to those who come from higher income homes. The broader definition of readiness recognizes that not all parents can provide the same opportunities or resources for their children that contribute to academic success. Communities and social agencies must help schools fill gaps and provide resources for families that lead to better outcomes for children.

The Success by 6 Initiative is one example of how communities are playing a larger role in getting young children ready for school. Sponsored by the United Way, Success By 6 is

> the nation's largest network of early childhood coalitions, focused on improving school readiness through community change. In more than 350 communities or states, Success By 6 (SB6) coalitions are changing the way things work so young children can come to school ready to succeed. (United Way of America, 2008, ¶1)

Even though there is the recognition that readiness involves communities, there still is an overwhelming amount of popular literature for parents that stresses readiness skills. The Executive Summary of the National School Readiness Indicators Initiatives (2005) articulated five domains of school readiness competencies for children to succeed in school:

1. physical well-being and motor development,
2. social and emotional development,
3. approaches to learning,
4. language development, and
5. cognition and general knowledge.

These domains generally provide the structure for organized checklists of readiness skills. Table 1 is an example of readiness indicators included on a Success by 6-sponsored calendar, distributed free to all parents in my local community, plus a few others I have added based on my experience working with young children. These skills are not just developed the summer before kindergarten begins—the development of these skills begins at (or, some even argue, before) birth.

Although the skills above are more narrowly defined, let's take a look at two broad categories of readiness skills: physical and motor development and cognitive and learning development. (Social and emotional development will be discussed in greater detail in Chapter 4.)

Physical Well-Being and Motor Development

In the readiness domain of physical well-being, we are referring to the child's physical health. Motor development is included because motor skills are indicators of natural growth and development. Breaking down the motor skills into specific tasks enables physicians and parents to notice developmental delays. Many readiness-screening instruments refer to motor development (both fine and gross) by specifying competency tasks (e.g., hop on one foot, grip a pencil, and so forth).

General Physical Well-Being

The physical well-being of the child pertains to the child's health and safety. In a broad-based definition, the community

Table 1
Kindergarten Readiness Checklist

Physical Well-Being

My child:

- ❏ Eats a balanced diet
- ❏ Gets plenty of sleep
- ❏ Receives regular wellness checkups
- ❏ Has had all of the necessary immunizations
- ❏ Runs, jumps, plays outdoors, and does other activities that provide exercise and help develop muscle tone in his or her larger muscles
- ❏ Works puzzles, scribbles, colors, paints, and does other activities that help develop small muscles and fine motor skills

Social and Emotional Foundations

My child:

- ❏ Has many opportunities to be with other children
- ❏ Begins to share
- ❏ Is learning to explore and try new things
- ❏ Is learning to work well alone and to do many tasks independently
- ❏ Is learning to finish tasks
- ❏ Is learning to use self-control
- ❏ Helps with family chores
- ❏ Is learning to use words to identify and express his or her emotions

Language and Literacy

My child:

- ❏ Has many opportunities to talk and listen
- ❏ Is read to every day
- ❏ Enjoys books and other reading materials
- ❏ Is learning about print and books
- ❏ Is learning to write his or her name
- ❏ Recognizes rhyming sounds

Numeration

My child:

- ❏ Is learning to count and plays counting games
- ❏ Is learning to identify and name shapes and colors

Cognitive Skills and Dispositions

My child:

- ❏ Is curious and motivated to learn
- ❏ Is encouraged to ask questions
- ❏ Is encouraged to solve problems
- ❏ Can follow simple instructions
- ❏ Notes similarities and differences
- ❏ Is encouraged to sort and classify things
- ❏ Has opportunities to draw and to be creative
- ❏ Has opportunities to listen to and make music and to dance
- ❏ Has opportunities to get firsthand experiences to do things in the world—to see and touch objects, hear new sounds, smell and taste foods, and watch things move

Note. Adapted from the United Way of Champaign County (2006–2007).

shares responsibility for the health of the child by keeping him or her free from drugs, crime, and poverty. Social service agencies should be working together to help parents without sufficient financial resources access the services they need to optimize the health of their children.

First and foremost, parents should take their children for annual wellness check-ups, timely dental exams, and vision screenings. In many states and communities, the local health departments provide vision and hearing screenings in preschools and daycare centers. Parents are required to immunize their children according to the recommended schedules defined by state health departments across the country. Almost every state requires a comprehensive physical before the child enters kindergarten. Some states now require dental check-ups.

The wellness check-ups inform parents about child development milestones and helps them be on the lookout for any behaviors or conditions that may seem abnormal. At wellness checkups, the doctor often asks about the normal routines for your child. The American Academy of Pediatrics sponsors a wonderful Web site called Medical Library. Visit http://www.medem. com/medlb/sub_detaillb.cfm?parent_id=10&act=disp to access several links to growth and development information for children. In addition, if you search for the term *developmental milestones* in the site's search box, you'll be able to access a variety of checklists to help you determine if your child's development is typical for his or her age.

Areas of growth include movement, hand and finger skills, language, cognition, and social and emotional growth. For example, according to the milestone list, 3-year-olds should be able climb, walk up and down stairs with alternating feet, kick a ball, run, and pedal a tricycle. Four-year-olds should be able to hop and stand on one foot, throw a ball overhand, and catch a ball most of the time. For fine motor skills, 3-year-olds should be able to turn a book one page at a time, build a tower of more than six blocks, and screw and unscrew jars. Four-year-old fine motor skills include being able to use a pair of scissors, draw circles and squares, and copy some capital letters. Cognitive skills for 3-year-olds include matching an object in one's hand to a picture in a book, sorting objects by shape and color, and completing two- and three-piece puzzles. Four-year-old cognitive skills include correctly naming some colors, recalling parts of a story, engaging in fantasy play, and understanding the concept of counting.

The complete lists may be found at the following Web site: http://www.med.umich.edu/1libr/yourchild/devmile.htm. You will notice that many of those tasks are commonly integrated into preschool activities and easily can be practiced within authentic contexts at home. There should be no reason to isolate the skills listed and "practice them." The milestones come from the children's naturally occurring activities and routines at the designated age levels.

Developmental milestones allow parents to compare their child to typically developing children. If for some reason the child is not able to do the types of things on the milestone checklist, then parents should begin asking the doctor questions. Not all children who do not meet the benchmarks on the developmental milestones are in trouble. My own child, because of his premature birth, was only 11 pounds at his first-year check-up. He was not walking yet! The doctor was not concerned because the growth curve was still going upward. He kept reminding me of where my child started. Height and weight are important indicators of growth—but do not be alarmed if your child is not yet on the charts. Healthy children grow at different rates, and doctors tend to look for positive curves of development over specific milestones. It is important however, to share with your doctor any concerns you have related to your child's eating or sleeping habits, as well as any other behaviors you notice that are not similar to what typical children should be doing at the same age. It is a fun activity for children to measure their height and weight on their birthday and keep a place in the house for them to see how much they have grown and continue to grow throughout their early years.

Other Developmental and Health Concerns

The development of speech is so closely related to the ability to hear that language delays often are associated with hearing problems. Abundant ear infections as infants may result in mild hearing loss. Therefore, regular hearing screenings are just as important to maintain as regular wellness check-ups.

One health concern getting much attention in the United States is autism spectrum disorder (ASD). In 2007, the Centers for Disease Control and Prevention's (CDC) Autism and Developmental Disabilities Monitoring Network found that about 1 in 150 8-year-old children in multiple areas of the United States had some form of autism spectrum disorder. Silverman and Weinfeld (2007) noted that although the numbers make it appear that the incidence of the disorder is on the rise, the criteria and definitions for diagnosis are not the same as that used in the past; therefore, despite increased attention to ASD, the recent prevalence of the disorder is not necessarily an epidemic.

Autism spectrum disorders are developmental disabilities that cause impairment in social interaction, communication, and attention. Often, children with these disorders display unusual behaviors and tend to focus on a sole topic of interest. Common symptoms of children with autism include self-stimulating behaviors, repetitive body movements, avoiding eye contact, withdrawn behavior, trouble relating to others, slow or nonexistent language development, and the repetition of words (called *echolalia*). These children also may be sensitive to noise, touch, smell, or taste. For example, they may not enjoy being hugged or caressed like other children. They may hold their hands over their ears when they hear loud music or loud talking. They also may not be able to tolerate specific foods or consistencies of certain foods.

ASD can and does occur in all races, genders, and socioeconomic groups (CDC, 2007), but tends to display itself in boys more frequently than girls. The CDC estimates that boys are diagnosed with ASD four times more than girls. Parents should know that autism spectrum disorders can be diagnosed as early as 18 months of age. The CDC notes that although "all children should be watched to make sure they are reaching developmental milestones on time, children in high-risk groups—such as children who have a parent or brother or sister with an ASD—should be watched extra closely" (2007, ¶ 4). The organization urges parents not to attempt to make diagnoses on their own, but to consult their health care professionals when a child displays the common warning signs of autism spectrum disorders. A list of potential signs, along with other information on ASD, can be found at http://www.cdc.gov/ncbddd/autism/symptoms. htm#possible.

Autism is considered a spectrum disorder, meaning its displaying behaviors occur along a continuum. Some children have more severe autism than others. Generally, the broad category of ASD includes five smaller categories: autism, Asperger's syndrome, pervasive developmental disorder–not otherwise specified (PDD-NOS), Rett syndrome, and childhood disintegrative disorder (National Institute of Mental Health [NIMH], 2008). Perhaps the most commonly discussed of these specific categories are classic autism and Asperger's syndrome.

There is a wide spectrum of autism disorders with some children being anywhere on that spectrum from low to high functioning. Asperger's syndrome is very similar to or may be the same as what is commonly called *high functioning autism*. Children with Asperger's syndrome may have impaired social interactions and delayed motor skill development. They typically are very bright and verbal, engage in conversation with adults, and focus on their interests, but have a difficult time relating to their peers.

Because autism is now becoming so prevalent, there are many resources for parents including books, Web sites, advocacy groups, and the National Autism Association. The purpose of including information about autism in this section is to be explicit about the importance of wellness check-ups. Children with developmental delays or diagnosed disorders can be helped significantly, if their symptoms are caught early, and early intervention programs are started. Although it is still unclear as to the causes of autism or Asperger's syndrome, there are effective early intervention programs, suggested diets, and other types of behavioral therapy treatments that parents may wish to learn more about by accessing resources on autism. Table 2 includes a list of potential resources for parents looking for more information on these disorders.

Table 2
Autism Resources

Autism Network International
http://ani.autistics.org

Autism Research Institute
http://www.autism.com

Autism Resource Network
http://www.autismshop.com

Autism Society of America
http://www.autism-society.org

Autism Speaks
http://www.autismspeaks.org

Council for Exceptional Children
http://www.cec.sped.org

Centers for Disease Control and Prevention:
Autism Information Center
http://www.cdc.gov/ncbddd/autism/overview.htm

National Autism Center
http://www.nationalautismcenter.org

National Information Center for Children With Disabilities
http://www.nichcy.org

National Institute of Mental Health: Autism Spectrum Disorders
(Pervasive Developmental Disorders)
http://www.nimh.nih.gov/health/publications/autism/complete-publication.shtml

Unlocking Autism
http://www.unlockingautism.org

Diet, Nutrition, and Exercise

Parents also have an important role to provide healthy diets for their children and teach them healthy habits and good nutrition. More and more of today's children are considered overweight or obese. In 2004, the American Heart Association estimated that more than 10% of U.S. children ages 2 to 5 were overweight, an increase from 7% in 1994 (Associated Press, 2004). Risks of being overweight or obese include coronary heart disease and juvenile diabetes. Parents can play a large role in helping maintain a healthy weight for their child's size and age, simply through changing nutrition and exercise habits.

The U.S. Department of Agriculture released a newly revised and updated version of its Food Guide for Young Children in 2005. My Pyramid for Kids combines colorful, fun activities for children to learn about healthy eating with detailed information for parents. In this pyramid, the USDA (n.d.) recommends the following breakdown of nutrients for children eating an 1,800 calorie diet (this figure may need to be readjusted for young children; to do so visit http://www.mypyramid.gov and enter your child's age, height, and weight to find the recommended number of daily calories and the amount of recommended nutrients from each food group):

- 6 oz. grains (half of which should be whole grains);
- 2 ½ c. vegetables;
- 1 ½ c. fruits;
- 3 c. milk (2 c. milk is recommended for children ages 2 to 8); and
- 5 oz. meat, beans, or other protein.

Some tips the USDA (n.d.) provides include incorporating whole-grain cereals at breakfast, providing dark green (broccoli and spinach) and orange (carrots and sweet potatoes) vegetables whenever possible, making sure juice is 100% juice (and going easy on juice in place of fresh fruit, as juice contains high levels of sugar), using lowfat or fat-free milks and cheeses, and making lean or lowfat meats, including chicken, turkey, and fish.

In addition to providing the oversight for a healthy child, parents also can demonstrate by example good practices and include the child in the discussion of why they are eating a well-balanced meal or why they buy cereal with low sugar content. Incorporating some of the above strategies, such as buying whole-grain foods, lean proteins, and dark green and orange vegetables, can benefit adult health, as well. In addition, parents can spend time with their children in activities that promote these behaviors.

In today's environment of media stimulation, it's easy to forget that children need plenty of physical exercise. The USDA (n.d.) notes that while adults are recommended to have 30 minutes of physical activity most days of the week, children need 60 minutes every day (or most days). Set a good example for your kids by promoting healthy exercise. It doesn't have to be running or going to the gym, either. Look for activities you can do as a family—go for a walk, play a game of tag or catch, or rollerblade or bicycle around the neighborhood. The USDA's Web site (http://www.mypyramid.gov/kids) provides great tips for incorporating fun activities that promote exercise, including:

- establish an exercise routine;
- make the next birthday party centered on a physical activity, such as skating or backyard relay races;
- set up a home gym with canned foods as weights and stairs instead of stair machines;

- get up and move during TV commercials; and
- give active games, toys, or sporting equipment as gifts.

And, most importantly, when your children do begin attending school, keep encouraging these healthy habits. Pack nutritious lunches, keep to your established exercise routine, and provide physical outlets for releasing stress, tension, or just muscles cramped from sitting most of the day.

Motor Development

My brother failed skipping in kindergarten. Although he is an accomplished artist now, one of the only stories I remember about him was the one my mother told us about his failure to know how to skip when he went to kindergarten. Was that important to be successful in kindergarten? Fortunately, skipping is not on every school's list of motor skills needed to enter kindergarten.

Motor development includes the growth of both fine and gross motor skills. Being aware of your child's motor development is important because it is indicative of how the brain, nervous system, and muscles work together. Children who lag behind in motor development may have some type of neurological impairment. One neurological disorder, cerebral palsy, is caused by damage to the motor control centers of the brain and affects a child's motor development.

Fine motor skills are movements that use the small muscles of the fingers, toes, wrists, lips, and tongue. Developing fine motor skills are essential to a child's progress in school because they include skills such as gripping a pencil, holding a pair of scissors, writing letters of the alphabet, opening jars, tying shoelaces, or building with small manipulatives such as LEGOs or Unifix cubes. Gross motor skills are the bigger movements that use the large muscles in the arms, legs, torso, and feet. Children use gross motor skills when they run, jump, climb, and ride tricycles. Most preschool playgrounds provide the equipment that gives children the opportunities to strengthen their gross motor skills. Parents also can support the growth of large motor skills by giving their children time to play on playgrounds with climbers, ladders, slides, and balance beams. In fact, most motor skills will be developed and strengthened by the normal play of young children without parents having to make an effort to build these skills.

Growing from tricycles to bicycles with training wheels is a rite of passage for young children. Some 4-year-olds are even starting to ride two-wheeled bikes. All of these new experiences are opportunities for children to learn skills that they will continue to use as adults. Include your child in the discussion of bicycle safety. When the child gets on a tricycle, provide helmets and go to the store with your child to pick out the right kind of helmet that is both comfortable and safe. Explain the important rule of staying on the same side of the road (a perfect opportunity to talk about right and left, oncoming cars, hand signals, and so forth) as he rides. When you ride with your child, you too should follow traffic lanes, give signals, and wear a helmet.

When parents give their children opportunities to draw, color, create, and play with their friends outdoors, they are giving them opportunities to use both small and large motor skills. However, if for some reason, their children do not get enough opportunities naturally to play outside, or be creative inside, there are growing numbers of "pee-wee" leagues that offer children opportunities to play sports at a young age. In my local community we have T-ball, soccer, dance classes, and swimming—all of which include children from 3 years old and upward. There are even some yoga classes and creative movement classes for young children in my area!

So, don't worry if your child cannot skip before he or she enters kindergarten. Skipping is not on every school's list of motor skills required. Here, just as an example, are a few motor skills required by one kindergarten (Westfield Community School, 2007). The child can:

- can play a simple group game,
- gallop,
- walk up and down stairs using alternating feet,
- catch a ball,
- bounce a ball,
- hop 6 feet,
- participate in different sports, and
- ride a tricycle.

Cognitive Development

We are all impressed with 2-year-olds who can say the alphabet, recognize letters, and count rotely to 10—but do they really know what those symbols mean? When most people think of getting young children ready for school, they are thinking about the academic skills that young children need for school. Cognitive development is much broader than that, and includes not just knowledge of the alphabet, concepts of print, or numbers—cognitive development is how children learn to think and make sense of their learning experiences.

Jean Piaget, one of the most famous cognitive development psychologists, based his research upon the experiences he had with his own children to define four stages of development: sensorimotor, preoperational, concrete operational, and formal operational. According to Piaget's stages of development, children who were 3 and 4 years old were in the preoperational stage, where they developed their language skills and were strongly egocentric (Feinburg & Mindess, 1994). According to Piaget, in the preoperational stage, children begin to use images and words to represent their ideas; but it is not until the concrete operational stage that they begin to use logic (7 years of age; Feinburg & Mindess, 1994).

There are many learning theories about how children acquire knowledge. Piaget's theories, longstanding in the literature of early childhood development, have more recently been challenged. As Feinburg and Mindess (1994) noted

> Many criticisms of Piagetian theory have been advanced. One argument focuses on evidence that concrete operational thinking is not an all-or-nothing quality. Children may be perception-bound in one situation and not in another. They may be conserving at one time and not at another. The critics of Piagetian theory argue that children's cognitive abilities seem to grow gradually rather than by stages. (p. 40)

Not all children go through such a hierarchical and linear path to development. In addition, some theorists believe that children can progress more rapidly through different stages with more adult or peer interaction and intervention. Vygotsky (1978) introduced the term *zone of proximal development* as the juncture where a child can grow from what he can do independently to what he can do with intervention by an adult or more capable peer. The zone of proximal development is where the child can be challenged to move beyond what he or she already knows to acquire new problem-solving skills or new understandings.

John Dewey championed "hands-on" learning and experiential learning. He often has been described as the father of progressive education, and espoused the theory of pragmatism—that children learn by doing. The University of Chicago Laboratory School where Dewey worked became famous for its innovative experiential learning (Feinburg & Mindess, 1994). Today, the notion that young children learn best by doing derives directly from the writings of Dewey.

Influenced by Piaget, Vygotsky, and Dewey, the field of early childhood education today promotes the idea that children learn by constructing their knowledge through their experiences with others, including peers and adults. Educators who adhere to a constructivist theory of learning believe that children already are thinkers and can apply thinking processes to make meaning of the world around them. The adults' role then is to help children connect what they know to what they are learning so they can use their thinking skills to make sense of their environment. According to Kohlberg and Mayer, "The educator's responsibility is to provide learning situations that challenge children's analytical and problem solving abilities, and to propel them toward higher-level thinking" (Feinburg & Mindess, 1994, p. 89).

Although many readiness checklists give specific academic tasks as prerequisites for entering school, it is more important that children come to school with sound cognitive foundations for learning and problem solving. The more and varied types of experiences we can give our young children, the more information they will have stored to connect to new ideas. Children need language skills to help them process information and articulate their thinking. Language skills are closely tied to literacy skills that include *listening, speaking, reading,* and *writing.* The more experiences children have, the more they also have to talk about. As will be discussed later in this book, talking with your child increases her vocabulary development.

Jablon and Stetson (2007) presented 10 tips for engaging teachers in conversation with their young students. These suggestions for holding conversations with young children also may be applied to parents:

1. Make sure both people get a turn.
2. Use facial expressions and comments.
3. Pause after you say something.
4. Describe what you see your child doing.
5. Ask your child to tell you his or her stories.
6. Talk about books.
7. Invite your child to teach you how to do something.
8. Ask open-ended questions.
9. Encourage self-expression.
10. Connect the conversation to the child. (p. 9)

To prepare children cognitively for preschool, parents need to interact with them in ways that will encourage them to express their ideas and their reasoning. The types of skills that children will use to identify letters, calculate number operations, and read with comprehension include the following:

- *Sorting by attributes*: learning to distinguish between what is different and what is the same.
- *Classifying*: putting all objects or concepts that are alike together, finding overlapping commonalities, and categorizing ideas (showing ability to generalize). The Venn Diagram is a great organizer to demonstrate to children

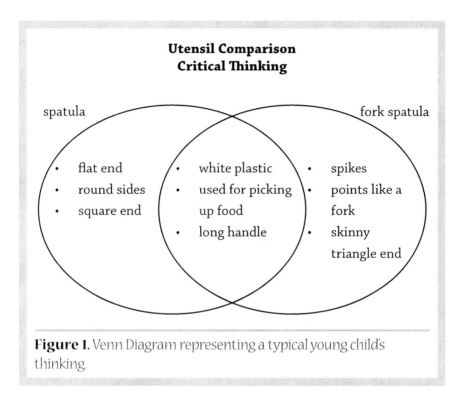

**Utensil Comparison
Critical Thinking**

spatula

fork spatula

- flat end
- round sides
- square end

- white plastic
- used for picking up food
- long handle

- spikes
- points like a fork
- skinny triangle end

Figure 1. Venn Diagram representing a typical young child's thinking.

how to classify their ideas or objects that overlap and share characteristics. Figure 1 shows a typical Venn Diagram for this age group.

- *Patterning*: finding and developing patterns—this helps children look for patterns in letters and words (e.g., rhyming, words that begin or end the same) and numbers and number series (e.g., what comes next, before, in the middle; what is added, subtracted).
- *Problem solving*: finding alternative ways to do something, work out a conflict, or think through a problem to identify possible solutions.
- *Disposition to inquire*: provide opportunities for children to ask and seek answers to their own questions.

Typical academic skills for preschoolers include tasks such as identifying colors and shapes, expressing their ideas through pictures that they draw or see, sharing their imaginative ideas through fantasy play, constructing with blocks or other manipulatives, listening to a book or story, telling their own story (which could be dictated to an adult), counting (possibly without one-to-one correspondence yet), recognizing or "tuning into" rhyming words, and a beginning awareness of environmental print or words and signs all around them.

Not all children will show an interest in reading or writing in preschool. Children can still develop their thinking abilities by building, sculpting, drawing, dramatizing, and playing. Obviously, at this age, parents should follow the interests of their children. Build in the types of thinking above into the way you interact with your child about his or her interests. If cars and trucks fascinate your child, use them to introduce new vocabulary, to sort by kind and purpose, to imagine where the cars and trucks could be going, to organize them by color and type and so forth. That way your child will connect his desire to learn about his favorite subject, with parents' support and interest. In the next chapter, I will share ideas of activities for parents to do with their young children across all of the readiness domains. Young scientists will find opportunities to experiment and explore their world, right in their very own homes.

Conclusion

Although it is tempting for parents and teachers to access resources (curricular packages and software) online that help children "practice" some of the skills mentioned in this chapter, the focus of this book is to share with parents ways they can enhance their child's readiness skills within authentic contexts—woven into the threads of family life. Parents may find they are providing these opportunities intuitively and naturally. This book may help to make these efforts more explicit and focused. Parents are the first, most important, and natural teachers of their young children. Remember, children are always ready to learn.

Chapter 2

What Can Parents Do?

SOFIA'S room was beautifully decorated in pink with her favorite ballerina lamp right next to her small bed. Stuffed animals and pink pillows were neatly arranged in one corner and white curtains trimmed in pink and green ribbon hung from the windows. In another corner sat a large refrigerator box, covered in hand-drawn pictures with a large hole cut out of one side, with pink tulle hanging from the opening. This was Sofia's castle—where she played like a princess. Some days it was dressed up to be the background for the imaginary stage on which she practiced ballet. On other days, it was filled with the pillows from the corner to create a retreat where she and her mom could read a book. Sofia, like many other children, took a simple item most adults would throw away and made it into a special place. To a young child, the actual item may not be interesting, but when a box becomes a house, a secret hiding place, a tunnel, a garage, a car, or a castle, your home becomes rich with creative thinking!

A child's first learning environment is the home. Therefore, it's important that parents create home settings that encourage the growth of the readiness skills, along with the growth of the child's individuality, discussed in the previous chapter. This chapter will look at various ways parents can incorporate learning into everyday home and play experiences.

Attending to the Physical Environment—Creating "My Space"

Before "MySpace" was common computer terminology, I always recommended to parents to create a space in their homes for their children to be messy, creative, and alone. This was the original version of "my space," where children could help choose what would be in their personal area, where furniture would be at their level, and where they did not always have to clean up their messes before coming to the dinner table. Things could be left "in progress." I highly recommended that all types of art materials would be available for children including colorful markers, crayons, scissors (child-appropriate type), pencils, assortments of paper (lined, unlined, scrap, construction, tissue, wrapping, colored, various sizes, textures, and shapes), glue, tape, stickers—you name it. If it could be used for creative purposes, it would be found there.

After visiting the preschools in Reggio Emilia, Italy, I discovered that what I was actually recommending for children was what the schools in Reggio Emilia included in every early childhood classroom, a mini-atelier (artist's studio). Students there are encouraged to express themselves by using a variety of natural and recyclable materials, framed as the "100 Languages of Children" (Edwards, Gandini, & Forman, 1993).

After visiting the Reggio Emilia schools several times, I have an even greater appreciation for the different types of materials that children might use and find interesting. I also increased my appreciation for the way materials were arranged, displayed, and organized within the children's environment. The crayons and markers were organized by colors and hues. Paints were provided for children to experiment with colors. The teachers might only make available shades of reds and oranges to represent the beautiful poppies found in the fields. Educators from Reggio Emilia refer to the environment as the "third teacher," meaning that children learn from their environment as well as from their families and teachers.

I now recommend to the parents of the students I work with at University Primary School to pay particular attention to the physical (as well as the emotional) environment in their homes. That includes making the child's physical personal space attractive and aesthetic, and using natural textures and colors to create a calm and inviting atmosphere for children to think and be creatively productive with their ideas. Although parents may be tempted to buy the cute primary colored furniture that many companies sell to represent *child-oriented*, I now recommend parents stick with neutral tones and natural materials that emanate warmth and harmony in the environment. Let family photographs and children's paintings and drawings add the color to the room.

Making sure your child has the supplies he or she needs to engage in the activities that interest him or her also creates a positive sense of "my space." Books on a variety of topics can be kept in this area, along with the art materials I recommended above. Children with a keen sense of science might wish to keep their collections (which may run the gamut from rocks, to bugs, to buttons) organized and catalogued in this space. Kids inclined to mathematics can be supplied with a variety of building materials and different types of rulers, protractors, and compasses, or other materials that can be used to measure objects. If your child is a natural writer, Nancy Peterson (2006) suggested keeping "workshop" components such as publishing materials (yarn, ribbon, construction paper, hole-punches, staplers, and cardstock), reference books (kids' dictionaries or other word collections), and organizational materials (file folders, paper trays, paper clips) on hand for kids to experiment not just with writing, but also with becoming authors. If you teach your young children how many of these supplies can be utilized, but also encourage them to explore the supplies on their own, you'll create an environment where children feel comfortable exploring their interests and expressing themselves.

Paying attention to the physical environment and to the spaces where children may come and go in your home is an important contribution to their well-being. Children must know that their environment is safe, clean, uncluttered, predictable, and calm for them to develop a sense of control and ownership.

Children can be taught to respect their environment and to have an appreciation for how it is set up, organized, or arranged. They can learn how to put toys away neatly, sort colors of markers, and put shoes away. Providing them with "places" to put things gives them confidence that they can independently find their belongings when they want to have access to them. Giving young children responsibilities and showing how everyone works together to keep the family going in harmony is important. Children want to feel a sense of belonging and they want to feel that what they do is important too. The physical environment contributes to the emotional well-being of your child and supports all of the other activities that you do with your child.

Media Overload

My first child had strict television limits because he was the only child in the house and I could control the television. He watched "Sesame Street" and family videos we rented from the video store. Once again, we controlled the movies he watched. One of the shows we let him watch was a Christmas special of Peter, Paul, and Mary (folk singers from my era) and to our amazement, he memorized every single one of the songs on the video (as long as he sang them in the same order). With his choices of videos so limited, he probably saw the video more than 20 times when he was young. No wonder he became a musician! We were the last family on the street to buy an X-Box, the machine that plays video games. My neighbor said our children were excited to go visit them because their kids had video games.

By the time my second child was 3, the video machines had become so complex, I couldn't even control them. Today there are infinitely more ways for children to get connected to media images than there were just 5 years ago, let alone 21 years ago. My children can play complicated simulation games on the computer, call their international friends, send a text message to anyone in the world, see thousands of video clips from all over the world on http://www.youtube.com, and use phones as alarm clocks, portable music players, and cameras.

Today's kids are surrounded by media—from TVs, to portable DVD players, to video conferencing, to cell phones and laptops. And, unlike kids a few generations prior to them, many of today's young children have become quite proficient navigating this media, even learning to explore the Internet to play their favorite games on Web sites like http://www.nickjr.com. According to the PBS Parent's Guide to Children and Media, a study conducted by the Kaiser Family Foundation found for children under the age of 6, 77% of children turn on the TV by themselves, 71% ask for their favorite videos, 67% ask for particular shows, 62% use the remote to change channels, and 71 % ask for their favorite videos (PBS Parents, 2008a).

The most significant ramification of "heavy" TV watching is less time spent in activities that are more valuable for children such as time reading with an adult, playing outside with a friend, or just learning to occupy oneself by being creative. According to the PBS Web site, "Regardless of their age, children from heavy-television households watched more television and read less than other children. Further more, children exposed to constant television were less likely to be able to read than other children" (PBS Parents, 2008a, ¶ 25).

Who knows what technology your 3-year-old will be exposed to in the next 5 years? How should parents respond? With caution! The American Academy of Pediatrics recommends that preschool-age children have no more than a total of 1 to 2 hours of high-quality TV or computer time each day (Illinois Early Learning Project, 2007).

In particular, parents should limit children's exposure to graphic images of violence. Although still being studied, young boys are more affected by the exposure to violence and become more aggressive than young girls after watching violent TV. The PBS Parents Web site (http://www.pbs.org/parents/childrenandmedia) summarizes the latest research on the effects of media on children of all ages. In addition, it has suggestions for parents to use media in various forms to enhance learning for their children. Parents can learn how to use computers, TVs, movies, video games, and advertising to their advantage. For example, on the PBS Parents Web site (2008a), suggestions are listed for how to "shape TV habits." This list includes:

1. Be choosy about the shows you and your child watch.
2. Watch TV when your preschooler does.
3. Prevent TV from replacing family time and active play.
4. Use TV shows and videos to enhance listening skills.
5. Avoid programs that show characters resolving conflict with violence.
6. Avoid programs that could frighten your child.

Common sense should guide parents' decision-making about the role the media plays in their children's everyday lives. Anything to excess is probably not in your child's best interests. In preschool, even violent cartoons are role-played on the playground.

TV no longer is the only media outlet young children are using regularly. Many young children are becoming proficient at using computers and the Internet. As the National Association for the Education of Young Children (NAEYC) noted, "As technology becomes easier to use and early childhood software proliferates, young children's use of technology becomes more widespread" (n.d.a, ¶ 2).

Take Maggie, for instance. She's 4 years old and spends a good deal of time at her great-grandmother's house while her mother works. Maggie's great-grandmother owns a MacBook, a laptop computer. Maggie has learned not only to open and turn on the laptop, but to navigate the mouse to find the "dock" where the computer's applications are loaded, to click on the icon for Safari (the Internet program on Apple computers), and to locate the bookmarks for her favorite Web sites. She plays games online that require both fun and practice of her numbers and letters. And, further, Maggie has learned to use her great-grandmother's computer as a communication tool, often asking her grandmother to sign onto iChat (the messaging system Apple employs) to check for other members of the family who are also online. Maggie can videoconference her family members and shows no hesitation talking into a camera built into the laptop, nor to the digital image of her family member on the screen. To her, it's like talking on the telephone.

PBS Parents (2006) offers strategies to help parents maximize their child's computer time, including:

1. Ask lots of questions as your child uses the computer.
2. Don't let screen time substitute for physical activity.
3. Introduce your child to software and Web sites that fan her creativity.
4. Get your child playing electronic games alongside others.
5. Find opportunities for your child to make decisions and try something new.
6. Keep one child or group from dominating choices.

A breakdown of each of these suggestions, with specific tips for implementing them in the home can be found at http://www.pbs.org/parents/childrenandmedia/computers-preschool.html. Further, Table 3 includes a list of kid-friendly Web sites that might help you get started with introducing your children to the suggestions included on the PBS site.

NAEYC (n.d.a) provides that considerable research has found technology to have positive effects on children's learning and development, but that the same research (Clements, 1994, as

Table 3
Web Sites for Young Children

Sesame Workshop
http://www.sesameworkshop.org

Nick Jr.: For Parents and Their Preschoolers
http://www.nickjr.com

StoryPlace
http://www.storyplace.org

PBS Kids
http://pbskids.org

KidsPsych
http://www.kidspsych.org

The White House for Kids
http://www.whitehouse.gov/kids

FisherPrice Fun for Kids
http://www.fisher-price.com

Seussville
http://www.seussville.com

Mister Rogers' Neighborhood
http://www.pbskids.org/rogers

Berenstain Bear Country
http://www.berenstainbears.com

cited in NAEYC, n.d.a) indicates that computers should only supplement traditional learning materials (books, blocks, writing materials, art materials, and so forth). Furthermore, just as computers and software can positively affect a child's developmental growth, it also can be misused, just like any other tool (Shade & Watson, as cited in NAEYC, n.d.a).

NAEYC (n.d.a) further maintains that developmentally appropriate software, when used correctly, offers opportunities for children to participate in collaborative play, learning, and creation. Software that allows children to be creative, interactive, and productive is by its nature more appropriate for young children than software where children are passive viewers. Although an abundance of software packages are available for purchase in most retail stores, NAEYC (n.d.a) cautions that a large number of such programs are not appropriate for young children. I've found some common computer programs such as Kidspiration, PowerPoint, iMovie, iPhoto (used to make photo albums), and Microsoft Word to be well-suited to expand upon a child's creativity when integrated into a child's day at school or at home as tools to use to express ideas—just as adults would use them!

RECIPE for Preparing for Success

The next section gives you six practical strategies that provide a RECIPE for integrating all of the readiness skills into your daily lives. If you are engaging in those strategies, your children will have a greater chance of being exposed to the types of experiences that get them ready for school.

Activities Across the Readiness Domains

I normally do not have the patience for following recipes, and do not usually believe in recipes for success. I know that individuals are different, and children are all unique. When cooking, I have a difficult time following recipes because I am always substituting ingredients for others that I do not have. I have learned that it is not always critical to follow the recipes as written. There is room for alternatives, and there is a margin of error.

However, recipes do provide guidance and yield practically the same results over time. The same can be true of the strategies proposed in my acronym of RECIPE. The techniques that comprise the acronym may work better for some families than others. They may be varied and altered to fit the available resources, and there is always margin for error—our children are resilient! Some techniques might work with one parent and child and might fail with the same parent and a different child. However, most of what will be described here cuts across all of the domains of skills we find listed on readiness checklists and in early childhood standards. The RECIPE is an acronym for the following strategies:

Read with your child.

Run **E**rrands with your child

Cook with your child.

Involve your child in activities that interest him or her.

Play, relax, and recreate with your child.

Explore with your child.

We'll explore each of these areas in greater detail in the sections that follow.

Read With Your Child

The early years are the most critical to language and literacy development. "One of the best predictors of whether a child will function competently in school and go on to contribute actively in our increasingly literate society is the level to which the child progresses in reading and writing" (NAEYC, 1998, p. 30). Both NAEYC and the International Reading Association developed a joint position statement entitled *Learning to Read and Write: Developmentally Appropriate Practices for Young Children*, which detailed best practices for the continuum of children's development of reading and writing based on research.

Most emphatically, the authors of the joint position statement express, "Experiences throughout the early childhood years, birth through age eight, affect the development of literacy," and "Failing to give children literacy experiences until they are school age can severely limit the reading and writing levels they ultimately obtain" (NAEYC, 1998, p. 31). Top on the list of things you can do to prepare your child for preschool and kindergarten is to read aloud with him or her *every* day. In some households, this happens naturally and routinely at bedtime. In other homes, finding time to read with one child may be complicated. It does not matter how it happens, but *do* find the time to read with your child. The advantages are both emotional and academic.

Emotionally, reading provides a calm, loving, and secure time that is shared between you and your child. Generally, reading takes place in a comfortable environment where both you and your child can relax and enjoy the book together. It is unhurried time and in some ways, the child has captured your full attention. It may be one of your only breaks from the hectic demands of everyday living, and therefore, the child may be getting a much calmer and loving adult during story time than at other times (like getting ready for daycare). Also, if reading can fit into the routine of your schedule (right before bed), the child has an opportunity to look forward to that time. He or she might finish other things (e.g., putting toys away) to make sure there is enough time before bed to have your full attention with a book.

The academic benefits are numerous. Reading with your child introduces her to concepts of print; expands her vocabulary; exposes her to conventions of books such as front cover, title, author, and illustrator; and opens up whole new worlds for her to explore. Discussing the book and having ongoing dialogue throughout the reading of the book keeps the child focused on the main ideas and concepts and enhances your child's vocabulary and critical thinking skills.

When you read a book to your child you are sharing the experience. You and your child can talk meaningfully about the characters, the setting, or the ending. You can encourage your child to think about alternative endings, or "What would happen if . . . ?" statements. Engaging your child in conversation about the book provides opportunities for your child to increase his literacy skills that include speaking, listening, reading, and writing. Your discussions about your book will give your child opportunities to ask questions and to listen to your responses to the same text.

For parents who are working with children who are beginning readers, I've summarized tips for making the most of reading time from the International Reading Association (1997):

- Follow words with fingers from left to right.
- Read books your child chooses.
- Point out key words and explain what they are.
- Ask questions as you read, "What's happening now?" "Where did he go?" or "What's she doing?"

- Answer your child's questions even if they interrupt the story.
- Ask your child to look at pictures for clues to meanings of new words.
- If your child gets stuck trying to read a word aloud, allow her to skip it and read to the end of the sentence. Ask her what she thinks the word could be.
- Choose another book if the child is not interested in the one you pick.
- Allow time to talk about the book after you read it. (p. 2)

Reading to young children enhances their language development. The more you talk to your child, the larger vocabulary he or she will have and the more verbal he or she will become. Take your child to the library often and choose books that rhyme or repeat familiar phrases. Children love reading the same books over and over. When children memorize books and "read them to you," celebrate their accomplishment. It demonstrates the natural progression to learning how to read. They are telling an enjoyable and predictable story, and it is fun for them to share!

Even when you think children grow out of being read to, continue to read aloud to them as long as they enjoy it. Children often enjoy reading a series of books by the same author because they love to become familiar with the characters or the images of the books. For example, my sons enjoyed the humor of the Amelia Bedelia stories by Peggy Parish. She was a maid who interpreted everything she was told to do literally. They could not wait to read the next story because they just knew Amelia was going to do something funny. Several links to lists detailing books and book series for this age group to explore is included in Table 4.

Table 4

Sources to Find Books and Book Series for Young Children

The following Web sites will be helpful in finding books geared to young children. In addition, your public library's children's librarian is a valuable resource for locating classic and contemporary favorites of other children.

Oakland Public Library: Books for Preschoolers
http://www.oaklandlibrary.org/links/kids/Booklists/
preschoolers.html

Carnegie Library of Pittsburgh: Kids' Page:
Books for Preschoolers
http://www.carnegielibrary.org/kids/booknook/
gradedbooklists/preschool.html

Fairfax County, VA: Book Lists for Tots
http://www.fairfaxcounty.gov/library/Reading/Preschl

Brooklyn Public Library: First Five Years:
Books for Preschoolers
http://www.brooklynpubliclibrary.org/first5years/read/
preschooler/books.jsp

Leading to Reading: Books for Preschoolers
http://www.rif.org/leadingtoreading/en/grown-ups/books/
booklist_preschoolers.mspx

You can choose to read aloud more complicated books than your children can read on their own. You can introduce them to great children's literature that provides opportunities for discussion. Children now have access to many videos and movies that are based on children's literature. Discuss how the movie version differs from the book and engage them in evaluative thinking as you ask them to tell you the similarities and differences, and why they like the book or the movie version better.

A great guide for parents to choose high-quality literature is to seek Caldecott and Newbery Medal winners (awarded by the American Library Association [ALA] annually). The Caldecott Medal is awarded annually to the artist of the most distinguished American picture book for children. The Newbery Medal winner is the author with the most distinguished contribution to children's literature. Although not all of the award-winning books are suitable for preschoolers, they are good places to start a collection for later reading. Most libraries and bookstores have displays or shelves of these books. In addition, a full listing of current and previous winners of the Caldecott and Newbery Medals is included on the ALA Web site: http://www.ala.org/ala/alsc/awardsscholarships/literaryawds/literaryrelated.cfm.

Enhancing Literacy Through Daily Activities

After reading to your child, probably the second most important thing you can do to enhance language skills and to advance literacy development is model reading, writing, listening, and speaking. Have many types of print materials available in your home such as newspapers, magazines, and books that you use. Engage your children in writing e-mails or letters to grandparents, making shopping lists, or leaving notes for older siblings.

All of the things that you do related to reading, writing, speaking, and listening are learning tools for your young children.

Encourage your children to tell and illustrate stories. Help the child label his or her drawing or write what the child dictates under the drawing. Print or type dictation on a computer using large font sizes so the child can "read" words that he remembers from telling you the story. Read the story back to the child and point to the words as you read them.

Prior to school, one of the most important goals for parents, caregivers, and teachers is to enhance children's exposure to and concepts about print. In lay terms, that means pointing out that printed words have meaning. Parents can do that by labeling important places or items in the house, or by pointing out the words on signs (e.g., Stop, McDonald's, and so on). My first clue that my younger son was learning his alphabet (when he was 2!) was when we drove past a K-Mart and he kept saying, "K." I did not have a clue what he was talking about until I noticed the sign.

Writing is an important component of emerging language and literacy. Give your children opportunities to "write" you notes or draw pictures. Do not worry about spelling. Remember that when your child learned to talk even his or her babbling elicited praise and smiles. Scribbling is the onset of writing, and when children put their pen to paper, they are trying to communicate. Parents need to value the act of communication and encourage fluency by empowering their children to spell the words like they sound. According to NAEYC (1998), "Studies suggest that temporary invented spelling may contribute to beginning reading" (p. 34). The research suggests that as children sound out their words, they think actively about letter-sound relationships.

Fostering Reading Enjoyment

Epstein (2007) stated, "Interest in reading cannot be forced on children. Fortunately, if they have positive experiences reading with adults, children will naturally be motivated to want to read" (p. 35). The following list of activities summarizes how to foster the enjoyment of reading in young children (Epstein, 2007):

- Read to children frequently.
- Create cozy and comfortable places where you can read with children and they can look at books by themselves. Provide stuffed animals and dolls for children to "read" to.
- Display books on open shelves, with attractive and colorful covers facing outward.
- Encourage children to select which books to read.
- Choose books that interest children.
- Let children see you reading for enjoyment and information.

There are countless other published lists of things parents can do to improve their children's literacy skills (see Table 5 for one example). Most include talking, singing, rhyming, reading, writing, and drawing in multiple ways with your children and with great enthusiasm.

The basic principle for strengthening literacy skills is to take advantage of natural circumstances and make children aware of their own sense-making of the printed word. Thus, instead of having your child practice writing his or her name, have your child sign his name on your birthday cards to Grandma and Grandpa or on his drawings that are decorating your house. Instill in your children the love of reading. Trips to bookstores and libraries

Table 5
Enhancing Literacy Tip Sheet

	Activities to Do With Your Child
Does your child like to play, run, or build?	• Be sure your child has time to play with other children. • Engage in conversation with your child. Use difficult language occasionally, and talk about what the hard words mean. • Play games with your child using letters, words, numbers, or counting. • Share rhythm and rhyme through songs and other chanting activities. • Take your child to grocery stores, parks, museums, art galleries, and community events.
Show your child how you use reading and writing in your everyday activities.	• When you make a list or leave a note for someone, or when you read the newspaper, a map, or a menu, your child sees that reading and writing are useful. • Talk with your child about signs, schedules, newspapers, and books, and encourage her to try reading them. • Read aloud to your child. • Visit the library, and help your youngster get a library card as soon as she can.
Encourage children to draw, write, and use books for fun and learning.	• Keep books, magazines, and games at home where your child can use them. • Keep materials for drawing and writing where your child can use them. • When your child draws, ask him to tell you about the picture. • Write his words down so he can go back to them and "read" them himself. • Show that you value and respect your child's efforts to read and write. • Remember that even scribbles are a step toward writing.

Note. Adapted from *Getting Ready to Read!* (Illinois Early Learning Project, 2007).

should be fun excursions that excite your children and give you an opportunity to observe their interests and choices in reading material. Books make great presents and demonstrate to your children how much you value books. Show them what a treat it is to discover a new one on the shelf.

Run Errands With Your Children

Running errands with your children exposes them to your community. They learn where hospitals, stores, and banks are located, and how many different people have occupations that help us in the community. They gain a sense of how long it takes to go to the doctor, grocery store, or veterinarian and the proximity of these places to their own home. However, running errands with young children is not efficient. I can remember shopping late at night just so I would not have to do it with my children in tow. If I went with my children, we would end up talking about everything in every aisle. They would undoubtedly grab the coupons from the dispensers that hung out just far enough to be reached by a child in the grocery cart. The cereal aisle seemed to be particularly geared toward the eye level of young children. All they could see were the sweet and sugary ones, and up high were the healthier kinds.

Much of our learning occurs through ordinary experiences. To understand this, try making a telephone call in another country! We don't realize what we have learned about our own environment because we live with familiarity. Young children gain that familiarity when they interact with their environment. Taking children on everyday errands helps them learn "ordinary" things that we may have forgotten we learned at one time ourselves. For example, we know which stores are open until when;

how to drive through a dry cleaner window, a bank, or a carwash; and how to shop for what we need (or do not need).

We often do not even know when we are learning new things. Children learn new things almost every waking moment of every day by observing, listening, touching, tasting, and interacting with their environment. We asked preschool students what parents did at the checkout counter, and some were convinced that the lady at the checkout counter gave their parents money. Well, it's true, they do sometimes give money back, but the students did not understand that their parents had given the cashier their money first. In other words, never assume that our toddlers or preschoolers understand what we take for granted.

Going to the Grocery Store

I once asked a kindergarten student where potatoes came from. He responded, "A box!" That is because he remembered going to the store and buying potatoes in a box and then cooking them with his mother for dinner. Children constantly are making connections to learn new things from their prior experiences. That is why it is important to give children many experiences for them to draw upon.

The grocery store experience not only gives children a sense of where we get our food, it also offers fabulous opportunities for children to engage in literacy and math skills. The grocery store fills our senses. Children have opportunities to see, feel, and smell differences in texture, color, and shape. The grocery store is such a fertile ground for literacy experiences that many early childhood curricula include the grocery store as a project or topic to study.

Going to the grocery store is like going to a literacy festival—there are signs and objects attached to those signs everywhere.

Children can read the lettuce sign, and then pick it up and feel it. Just spend a few minutes in front of the different types of lettuce, and talk to your child about the differences in color, feel, and taste. Experiment with your child and find out which types of lettuce he likes. Have him pick a different type each time. In the spring, try growing different types of lettuce at home and see which grows best with your climate and soil.

As you purchase items on your grocery list, verbalize your reasons for making certain selections. Children can begin to notice similarities and differences between the objects and where they are located. Have your child notice how things are categorized—frozen things in one area, cans in another, and fresh produce in another area of the store. When you go to a different grocery store, have the child make predictions of what he might find based on what he knows about the first grocery store. If your child has any type of food allergies, teach him to read labels. Tell your child what you are looking for when you read the label. When you get home, have the child help you put the cans on the shelves, sorting by categories of foods, vegetables or fruit, for example.

Mathematical readiness skills include discriminating colors, shapes, and sizes. The grocery store has many opportunities for you to point out how foods are sorted by colors, shapes, and sizes. There are abundant ways that parents can integrate math skills into a simple shopping trip to the grocery store. Have your children notice the price signs. Have them estimate how much something weighs (e.g., bags of beans, potatoes, meat, and so on). Show the child how you put the produce on the scale. Have him or her pay attention to the way the people at the meat or deli counter weigh what you purchase.

Give your child a small amount of money for him to choose a treat at the store. Show him many items that would equal the amount of money you have given to him. Let your child hold the coupons and help you look for the coupon item (having to match this is no easy task!). For children who are interested, point out sizes of containers and the prices relative to the size. Give them an economic education and talk about what may be a "good deal" or a "better deal." Children will be interested in which products cost more or less money. Have the child notice the cash register and the scanner systems. Explain what happens as you give the cashier money and he or she gives you change in return (this lesson alone is worth paying in cash once in a while).

There also are many science lessons in a trip to the grocery store. Discuss what foods you consider to be healthy and have your child help you look for them. Point out how carrots sometimes come with their tops on, while other times they are precut into various shapes and sizes. Talk to your children about how particular vegetables grow in the ground. Experiment with tasting different fruits and vegetables that may be unfamiliar to them (e.g., mango, kiwi, rhubarb). Provide choices for your child within food group categories. For example, ask him or her if he or she would like pasta or rice, green beans or peas, or peaches or tangerines for dinner. When you serve dinner, tell the other family members that the child you took with you to the store helped to plan the dinner menu, giving your child a sense of self-worth in the family's daily operations.

Trips to the Bank

After realizing that you have to have money to pay for groceries at the store, a natural question might be "Where does the money come from?" Going to the bank offers so many possibilities to talk with your child. At the drive-through window there are red and green lights. There are cameras and automated buttons. The bank errand lends itself to learning many literacy and math skills. If children have their own piggy bank where they collect change, it is a fun activity to predict how much the change is worth once it is counted.

Just watching their parents get money gives them experiences that they then connect to later academic learning. When they have to identify differences between pennies, nickels, and quarters, they will have memories of taking their change to the bank and getting dollars back. If you give your children $1 to spend, they will soon learn what $1 is worth. Having children notice the differences in the coins and letting them separate the change they find around the house is a great way for them to start identifying the shapes, sizes, and values of the coins, giving them a leg up on math learning later in their schooling.

Shopping at the Mall

My first near heart attack occurred when I lost my younger child under a skirt rack at a local department store. The next one occurred when he came home one day and told me Grandma had been lost at K-Mart. Taking your child shopping is no easy task, and so why would I recommend it? Shopping—getting things we need—is part of our lives. It is one of the best places to teach values and common sense. My favorite shopping trips were taking my young children to buy presents for other people (after I was sure they could not make them themselves). They learn to care and think of others.

When you take them to buy their own clothes, they can learn about sizes and values. They see firsthand how they have grown. At the shoe store, they can watch the salesperson use the special measurement tool that measures shoe sizes. They can begin to read numbers of sizes on racks and clothes. They can be taught what size they are and what to look for. They also have some say in what they wear if they get to choose it at the store. They learn that they cannot buy everything they might want to buy. My son, when he was about 5, once said (loud enough for others to hear), "Mom, go to the back where the sales are!"

When children are at a shopping mall they see all types of people and they learn that they are part of a larger community. They also learn how to tell the lady in the shop that their grandmother is missing! As you warn your children to stay close to you, you also give them practical advice. You begin to teach them how to seek help when they need it. Trips to shopping malls are opportune times to teach children vital information about themselves they can give to others if they are lost. Most young children can easily learn their parents' full names, and some are able to remember phone numbers and addresses to give to adults in case of an emergency.

When you have a whole string of errands, and you're ready to pack your children in the car, if at all possible, give them a choice of where they go first. (You can always narrow the choices down to the two that are the most convenient for you.) That small gesture increases their interest in the errands and lets them know that they, too, have a say in the schedule of the day. As you talk about your errands and you go from one to the next, they will get the sense of accomplishment that they are completing important tasks. They will have lots to talk about upon their return home.

Other Errands

You may discover there are other places that your children love to go based on their interests. Going to the hardware store was one of my oldest son's favorite places because he had an intense interest in tools. There he could see many different kinds and sizes of wrenches, hammers, and screwdrivers. My second son preferred a store where he could play with the video games that we did not allow at home. Going to Best Buy was like going to a toy store for him. So, although we were prone to losing him at a discount store, we knew right where he was at the electronics store—his hands were on the controls.

Just paying attention to your children's interests as they go through various stages by giving them time in their favorite places helps them feel valued and somewhat independent. Their favorite errands can be on your list too.

Cook With Your Child

Yes, the kitchen can be a dangerous place for a child. But, it also can be a rich educational environment. My younger son said his first words, "Hot, hot, hot!" as I was holding him and stirring a pot of noodles. (His legs probably did feel the heat of the steam!)

Most of the time when you're in the kitchen with your children, you probably lead them to the one cabinet they are allowed to be in—the pots and pans. I often sat my first child in front of the cabinet and opened the door while I fixed dinner. He stayed busy down there taking pans out, putting different sizes of lids on various sizes of pots, and trying to fit them all back in the cabinet. Sometimes he actually put the right size lid on the right size pot and screamed with delight. Once in a while, I gave him wooden spoons and then I had a "drum set" that accompanied my dinner preparations.

But, preferable to having my children with me when I cooked, was having them *help me* cook. As I admitted before, I seldom followed recipes—mostly because I rarely made food from scratch. But, I did love following recipes for children, and especially making dinosaur cookies (while my son went through the dinosaur phase). We also made tool and airplane-shaped cookies to fit my sons' various interests. Cookie cutters can be bought in a variety of shapes and are useful for teaching young children shapes and object names in a fun manner. You can even buy number and letter-shaped cookie cutters and spell your child's name or teach him or her to count.

Some early math skills that can be incorporated into any cooking activities include counting with one-to-one correspondence, comparing more and less, sorting by sizes and shapes, recognizing patterns, and exploring parts to whole relationships. Cooking activities are far superior to workbook-type activities that ask children to color the page with a 5 on it and trace the letter. Children can learn one-to-one correspondence in counting when you ask them to take out two eggs from the refrigerator or pour two teaspoons of salt. As you count with them, they associate the egg or the teaspoon with the number you are calling out. They learn size relationships and begin to understand purposes for measurement when you ask them to help you pour one fourth, one half, or two thirds cups of milk.

In addition to mathematical thinking, children gain other important readiness skills from cooking. They gain physical strength and fine motor skills when you ask them to help roll the dough and cut out specific shapes. They see how ingredients can be combined to make their favorite foods, and they start paying attention to those ingredients. They can help you find them on the shelves of the grocery store. They learn to read food labels and compare their sizes. If you are measuring one cup of sugar from a pound of sugar, you can ask them to hold both of them and tell you which feels heavier. They can predict how many cups of sugar are in the bag. They can see when you use hand tools and electronic tools in the kitchen and be exposed to numerous kitchen devices that begin to build their vocabulary (e.g., mixer, blender, cheese grater, potato peeler, bread making machine, and so forth). If you have time, you can rewrite the recipe into a format that helps them follow along. For example, you can draw icons to represent 3 eggs, 2 cups of flour, and so forth. Following a recipe is a wonderful example of reading for a purpose. You can then keep a record of all of the recipes that you do with your child and put these into a memory book. The child will be reading his recipe book as one of his first independent reading books.

Besides baking cookies, what else can your young children help you cook? There are an abundance of recipe books for children. Some have favorite recipes that go along with children's books. Five such books include *Green Eggs and Ham Cookbook* (Brennan, 2006), *Roald Dahl's Revolting Recipes* (Dahl & Dahl, 1997), *Roald Dahl's Even More Revolting Recipes* (Dahl & Dahl, 2003), *The Storybook Cookbook* (MacGregor, 1980), *The Little House Cookbook* (Walker, 1989), *Mary Poppins in the Kitchen* (Travers, 2006), and *The Boxcar Children Cookbook* (Blain & Deal, 1991). Other kid-friendly cookbooks include *The Fairy Tale Cookbook* by Sandre Moore (2000), *Kids Cook 1-2-3* by Rozanne Gold (2006), and *Williams-Sonoma Kids in the Kitchen* by Stephanie Rosenbaum (2006).

If you want your child to explore shapes, try designing his or her peanut butter sandwiches into triangles, circles, and parallelograms, yes parallelograms! Expose your child to shapes that are beyond what is expected in that preschool classroom. When you talk about the subtleties of the shapes, and the differences in the angles and sides, he or she will draw upon these experiences for future more formal math instruction later. But, he also will remember that the eyes that you cut into his bologna sandwich were round, and that the sandwich was shaped like a triangle. Repetition helps children remember shapes, and once your child can tell you what a triangle is, breaking the routine challenges him or her further.

Other cooking ideas include having children "make" their lunches, constructing sandwiches, salads, and of course, many, many desserts. Experimenting with desserts continues to be a favorite past time in our household. With every ingredient being a favorable one, how can you go wrong? Your children too, will enjoy concocting their own recipes, mixing colors, and having fun taking taste tests, all the while giving them the freedom to explore (not waste!) and try new foods.

Cooking with your child not only strengthens academic skills, but the time you spend together is precious. Both of you share responsibility for whatever yummy food is prepared. Both of you gain a sense of accomplishment for completing a task. And, both of you have memories of working together toward a common goal. Cooking is yet another way to empower your child to be successful.

Involve Your Child in Activities That Interest Him or Her

You may find life complicated enough without having to think of outside activities for you and your children. Especially if your children are in childcare, you may think they have all of the socializing they need and that they just need to come home and spend quality time with you. In some cases, that might be true. But, some children need opportunities to be with other children with similar interests. That may mean joining a local activity such as creative movement classes or a children's soccer league.

Tapping into your children's interests are fundamental opportunities for you to expand their learning and for you to show that you value and respect their ideas. Some children will have an interest in one thing and then move on to another. I can remember several themed birthday parties based on my own children's interests. Fairly common interests at this age include dinosaurs, construction vehicles (e.g., diggers, backhoes, dump trucks), specific dolls (e.g., American Girl, Barbies), and other toys that are marketed for parents to purchase collections. Having a few children to your house who share those interests will provide an outlet for play that brings two goals together: to increase cooperative play and to provide time for your child to enjoy his or her interests.

The other way you can encourage and increase the scope of your child's interests is to introduce him to related areas. For example, take your child to a museum, a pet store, or an exhibit (e.g., old cars, trains, racecars). These experiences, even though they are built around specific interests, encourage your child to expand those interests. For example, on a trip to the museum to see dinosaurs, you might point out other interesting animals or the ways in which the habitats are constructed to look real in the museum exhibits. When you take your child to see the electric trains, he might notice how the exhibit has the train going through little villages with models of people doing things we do not necessarily do today. A conversation about how trains and our lives have changed may spark a whole other area of interest.

Do not stress over the fact that your child may be interested in only one thing at a time. Some children just naturally focus with intensity on one interest at a time. However, be alert for opportunities to share their interests by providing time to explore them together. Vacations can be planned with your preschooler's interests in mind. If your 4-year-old son has a huge collection of racecars, and talks about cars all of the time, it might be reasonable to take him to see a racecar museum or a NASCAR track. Even if you think he may be too young to remember his visit, the conversations that you have with your child when you take him there will open up whole new areas for learning and will provide experiences for connections later as he matures.

I am not suggesting that you overextend your children's activities. But, be attuned to their interests. Be on the lookout for free events or activities that are offered in your community that your child would enjoy. It is important to connect children not only to other children with similar interests, but also to events and activities that occur outside their immediate homes. Do not wait for children to be old enough to behave. They learn appropriate behavior by becoming engaged and involved and watching how other children their age respond to their environment.

Play and Relax With Your Child

Playing and relaxing with your child sounds easy because you do not always have to plan it. Your children naturally will engage you in play as soon as you sit down to have a quiet moment for yourself! So, why play with your child? What does it mean to play and relax? You are always reaching for a delicate balance between the amount of time you engage in their play (and possibly change the direction of it), and the amount of time you sit nearby and listen carefully, observe what is going on, who is taking the initiative, and who gets frustrated more easily than others. You also need to delicately balance the time when you are truly relaxing with your child (enjoying music or books together) and engaging in some form of play. Hopefully, there will be moments when you can both play and relax at the same time.

Imaginative Play

Encourage imaginative play because it enhances your child's creativity and develops language skills. Put together a box of old clothes and accessories so your child can dress up. Include career-based accessories such as stethoscopes or fire hats and neutral clothing such as old white shirts, which can become anything from Dad's suit shirt, to the dentist's lab coat. Collect boxes and other recyclable objects for your child to turn into props. Encourage your child to explain to you who (or what) he or she is pretending to be. Your child's imaginative play may seem nonsensical to you, but listening to the images and the stories that your child creates provides you information about your child's perspectives, interests, or concerns.

When you tune in to your child's play, you learn a great deal about him or her. Often, children dramatize events that are significant to them. They may have imaginary characters that do things that they cannot do. You may be able to add your own characters and build their vocabulary by giving words to the images and sounds they are creating.

Their creative dramatic play is an opportune time to enhance language and literacy development. For example, as the child creates noises with his airplane and zooms it over your head, you may describe the scene for him, "Wow, look at your airplane soar over my head!" You may find your child enjoys role-playing and dramatizing the same stories over and over again. Gently, you might probe his stories to see if he has different characters that do unusual things, thereby adding on and building details into his stories. You could ask, "Who is with you? What is he doing in the airplane now?"

Take photographs of your children playing and then have them tell you what they were doing when they revisit the printed photographs. Sequence the photographs together so they see how their stories have a beginning, middle, and end. You may have to help your child negotiate his dramatic play with a friend by offering alternative roles for the friend to play. Dramatic play is open-ended and allows your children's creativity and interests to go in unlimited directions. Provide as many open-ended types of toys as possible that allow your children to play in areas of their interest. Construction-type materials are great toys because children enter the task at their own level. If they can play with blocks in some location of the house where they do not have to clean them up every night, then they can revisit their structures the next day and build onto them, adding more details and complexity. This teaches children that long-term engagement builds more complex structures that generally lead to more detailed imaginative play. They may add toy cars or toy airplanes to their block structures. It also is quite common for children to add toy animals to their block structures, building different rooms or habitats for the animals, replicas of ones they may have seen at a zoo.

Encourage your children to represent what they see in the world around them with blocks, LEGOs, or other constructive materials. For example, if you and your children recently have been to the bank, have them build the bank out of the blocks. If they love going to Dad or Mom's office, have them make the block area the office. Blocks, LEGOs, clay, play dough, K'nex, and other similar toys that promote creativity provide an arena where children can express their creativity and parents can provoke their thinking to challenge their patterns of play to promote learning new vocabulary, new forms of expression, and new ways of interacting with the materials.

Note that you don't have to necessarily go out and purchase materials for your child to imaginatively play with. Often, children find simple joy in creating new objects from old materials. Keep old boxes—large boxes can become playhouses, forts, or schools and smaller boxes can become treasure chests, bricks for building, or bodies for robots or play cars. Paper towel and toilet paper rolls, along with long wrapping paper rolls, also can be molded to create shapes traditional blocks forgo, such as semi-circles or tunnels and tubes.

Play Indoor and Outdoor Games With Your Child

Winter months in many places can be cold and dreary. But, spicing up a winter evening with an inside game that everyone can play generates both learning and fun. Charades is a favorite indoor game that you can play with your whole family. Depending on the age of your children, you can act out animals, storybook titles, or favorite television shows and movies. Bingo is another game that can be geared toward different age levels. You can make your own Bingo cards to suit the level of learning that is appropriate. Bingo cards can include numbers up to 10 or numbers in the thousands. They also can be names of famous people or people in your extended family (with icons or photographs if you wish to help the beginning or nonreader). Your children will enjoy making a contribution to the game.

Card games also are fun. Playing Go Fish or War (where the person turning over the highest number takes the card) can teach children numeral recognition skills. There are now family interactive games that involve asking questions and then seeing vignettes from a DVD to help answer them. If you choose perhaps one night of the week when the family will play games together, it will give your child something to plan for and look forward to. Also, giving your child a choice is another way you can build his confidence to control part of his environment. We'll discuss two common types of games below.

Board Games. Board games are more structured and generally have more rules to follow. There are several family board games that encourage counting skills, taking turns, and figuring out some strategy—all great readiness skills for preschool. The possibilities are too numerous to name here, but children will enjoy going with you to pick out board games, and they will enjoy helping to set them up. Many more traditional games like Monopoly and Scrabble have children's versions, many of which play on children's favorite characters, creating another level of interest in the game. It actually is easier for children to learn these board games by playing with adults than other children, because adults generally follow the rules. When children begin to play board games with other children, rule negotiations take center stage—as long as children learn to play together, compromising certain rules is part of the play. Parents should be relaxed about "winning" and emphasize the fun they can have by playing no matter who wins.

Outdoor Games. Although outdoor playground equipment is always fun, when left to their own devices without such equipment at hand, children often become very creative in initiating their own outdoor play. Games of pretend scenarios, like the traditional "cowboys and Indians" or "cops and robbers" games, are always popular. However, children have been inventing and playing their own outdoor games for centuries. In 1744, John Newbery's *Little Pretty Pocket-Book* included a ball for boys and a pincushion for girls, along with listings of games common to children of that era (Demers, 2003). Several of them still exist today (baseball, for instance).

Outdoor games that can be played with young children include the following list with brief instructions. All of these games require nothing more than the children themselves and a large space. All of them have many variations, so you can go with the versions here, use one from your childhood, or find another version online.

- *Red Light/Green Light*: One child is designated as the stoplight. He or she turns his or her back to the group, all of whom stand along an invisible line (an equal length from the stoplight). The stoplight shouts "Green light!" and the children run toward him or her. When the stoplight shouts "Red light!" all of the children must stop. The game continues until one child reaches the stoplight first. He or she is the next stoplight.

- *Hide and Seek:* A perennial outdoor/indoor favorite, all of the children except one hide, while the seeker counts to an arbitrary number set by the group. Once the seeker reaches the set number, he or she must try to find the other children, all of whom my leave their hiding places and attempt to run to the seeker's home base before they are found.

- *Simon Says*: Young children love this game, and it's great for building their language comprehension too. One child is chosen to be Simon, and the others stand (or sit) before him or her in a semicircle or straight line. Simon gives directions to the other children, prefacing the directions with "Simon says . . ." The object is for Simon to slip in directions in which he does not say "Simon says . . ." The child who follows the directions without the prefaced phrase is out of the game.

- *Tag*: Tag can be played in a number of varieties. Simple tag designates one child as "It," who must chase the other children. Once he or she tags another child, that child is now "It," and the game begins again. Many children play a version called *Freeze Tag*, wherein the tagged child must freeze in place until a friend who is not "It" tags him or her. The goal for "It" in this version is to tag and freeze all of the other children.

- *Mother May I?*: One child (playing the mother) stands away from all of the others, who stand in one straight line. The child playing mother calls on each of the other children in turn, instructing them to take a certain number (and size, and even type!) of steps forward or backward. The other child must ask, before he or she moves, "Mother May I?" The mother can choose to say yes or no based on his or her whim. The goal is to be the first child to get to mother.

- *Duck, Duck, Goose*: All of the children sit in a circle, except one ("It"), who walks around the outer edge of the circle, touching the other children on the head and labeling them as a duck or a goose. If you are labeled as goose, your job is to catch the other child, chasing him or her around the circle, before he or she can take your seat. If the goose is unable to catch the other child, he or she is "It" for the next round. If the child playing "It" gets tagged by the goose, he or she must sit in the center of the circle, commonly called the *mush pot*, until another child is tagged to replace him or her.

One source for finding multiple games (and their variations) online is http://www.gameskidsplay.net, which includes a lengthy alphabetical listing of common games.

Other games children enjoy include those that need a little more equipment, such as jump rope rhymes or double-dutch, hop scotch (some variations require beanbags or small objects to be thrown into the squares), sack races, three-legged races, kickball, wiffle ball, or four square.

Whatever your child's favorite game, the important thing is that you encourage imaginative, cooperative play. Often, you'll find that your older children (and/or other family members) will enjoy playing too!

Explore With Your Child

The Valentine's Day ice storm of 1990 was horrific and caused some of the worst damage to trees in Illinois history. My oldest son was 3 ½ at the time. Schools and businesses closed down because it was too treacherous to travel and power was out across the city. The icy landscape was beautiful. My son and I bundled up, took a camera, and went out exploring. To this day, my child remembers how we picked up large, heavy icicles and brought them back to our freezer so that we could enjoy them the following July when the weather turned hot. We took pictures of grass almost crystallized with ice on every blade. When daycare resumed, my son shared his ice storm adventures with his friends and teachers.

Exploring the world together is an explicit way of valuing lifelong learning. It gives children the message that parents are learners too and there is so much in our environment to learn about. It teaches children to observe carefully and to appreciate their natural environment and changes in that environment.

You do not need a major disaster to begin exploring. Take time out on your daily walks to take pictures of ordinary things, collect objects or artifacts that you find along your route, and have a place for your child to draw or write about them later. This is an opportunity to teach children to think like scientists—just as most scientists keep lab notebooks of their experiences, so too can your child record what he or she has seen and done. Allow your child to personalize her journal or notebook, decorating the cover or building one from construction paper, string, and a hole punch, with notebook or white paper in the middle. If she takes pride in her creation, she'll certainly take pride in recording and sharing what she's learned.

Good scientists also share what they have found in their explorations. Have your child dictate to you a story about what he saw or what happened along the way. Turn these dictations into little adventure books that you can give to grandparents with photographs or your child's drawings. These adventures build language skills as children expand on their experiences through talking and writing.

Most communities have many places to explore, including older homes or different architecturally designed neighborhoods, museums, libraries, post offices, and parks. We often think of exploring these places when we visit different cities. But, many of these opportunities are available in your own city.

Try exploring parks you usually do not go to and have your child tell you what she likes or does not like about them. You will gain insight into what your child finds fun and interesting and your child will have a natural opportunity to compare and contrast play environments—something children know lots about. Going to outside parks is an opportune way for children to develop their gross motor skills. They naturally will want to climb on the apparatus and try out all of the slides, swings, or ramps. Generally there will be other children at the park, giving your child opportunities to build social competencies by playing with other children.

Exploring with your child need not be expensive. If you feel that *you* need a change of environment, drive to a nearby town and discover a playground or a park together there. Take a picnic lunch and you and your child will share an adventure that she can talk about for a long time.

Museum Visits

All of the literature on readiness suggests that taking your children on trips is beneficial. Why? Trips broaden your children's experiences and give them more to talk about with you, once again encouraging growth in vocabulary development and literacy in general. A gentle caution on museum exhibits is to not make your children "take it all in" on one visit. Do one part of the museum at a time and then come back to explore more. Sometimes we can overwhelm children with what we want them to know and do.

All-day museum visits often present tiring experiences, rather than engaging and joyful ones. It is a good idea to prepare your child for some things he or she might see. Letting the child make predictions and then having him compare his predictions to what he actually saw is another good way to engage him in inquiry. Let the trip to the museum be led by some of his questions, instead of something that is ruled by adults. When the child says he is not ready to leave the museum or that he wants to see more, then you know you've been successful at instilling a positive attitude toward inquiry and learning.

If you are looking for a museum to include on your next family vacation, consider visiting the Association of Children's Museums Web site (http://www.childrensmuseums.org). This site includes a state-by-state listing of the nation's children's museums, designating which have been accredited by the organization. However, you need not go far to have a quality museum experience with your child—most communities also have children's museums or children's programs at local museums and zoos that can serve the same learning purposes.

Exposure Versus Understanding

It is not necessary that children understand everything that is presented to them. Many times we as adults do not understand everything we read or see. The experiences that you are exposing them to, however, enables them to have a broader knowledge base so that they have more prior experiences to build upon and make connections to new things that they are learning. Thus, do not always determine whether or not an experience is worthwhile if you think your child will not understand it. Some experiences are worthwhile just for exposure purposes. A trip to the art museum is a case in point. You may want to visit a special exhibit on a famous artist in the art museum and you think your child would be too young to appreciate it. On the contrary, taking your child with you for an exhibit focused on one artist gives him the exposure to that artist. Although he may never understand as much as you do about that artist from that one visit, the next time he goes to see an art exhibit on another artist, he will be able to talk about similarities and differences, what he liked and what he didn't like, and maybe even make some connections between the artwork he saw at the museum and other artists that illustrate his storybooks.

Never underestimate the role that exposure plays in facilitating other learning experiences. My oldest son came home from taking his ACT tests excited because one of the reading portions was about the physics accelerator at CERN, a government physics laboratory in Geneva, Switzerland. My husband, who is an experimental physicist, and I lived in Geneva while he was doing his postdoctoral work (before we had children). My son had heard us talking about our experiences, and vicariously through our conversations became familiar with knowing that CERN had an accelerator. This exposure gave him a huge advantage to other students reading that same passage who might not be able to make any connections with the terminology, thereby slowing down the comprehension of the piece.

In-House Adventures

You do not even need to go out of your house to share the spirit of exploring. My husband often had the evening ritual of giving our sons a bath. One night, I kept hearing the water go on and off. I could not imagine what was taking so long upstairs, or why after I thought they were out of the tub, I heard the water come on again. Finally, I went upstairs to find out that they were experimenting with the drain. Over and over they filled the tub and watched the "tornado" go down, finding out if it always spiraled the same direction.

The home also is an ideal place to explore simple machines and other tools or inventions we cannot live without. Show your children how doorknobs and locks work. Introduce them to the simple machines we use every day, such as the wheels on their model cars (and Mom's or Dad's car) or the screw used to close the jelly and peanut butter jars.

You also can set up great adventures inside your house. For example, for parents who do not appreciate camping in the great outdoors, setting up a tent in the living room is a great simulation. Making s'mores in the microwave and telling stories by flashlight in the tent can provide a unique experience in the comfort of your own home.

Finding ways for children to explore both the familiar and the unfamiliar enhances your children's dispositions to be inquisitive, to persist in finding out answers, and to be experimental—all skills that help to build competent problem solvers. Skills on readiness checklists that include attitudes toward learning (e.g., asks questions, solves problems, notice similarities and differences, sort and classify, has many opportunities to talk and listen) are naturally practiced within the authentic context of exploring and adventures.

Conclusion

In this chapter, I have shared a RECIPE for successfully integrating readiness skills into daily life with a preschooler. I am quite sure there are several different "recipes" for giving young children opportunities to develop academic, as well as social and emotional competencies. What is most important to remember is that you want to give your children the *love* for learning and the support to *inquire* and be *curious* about the world around them. Learning new things every day is not only a goal for your child, but one for parents, as well. Parents who love to learn alongside their children are providing the foundations for a rich beginning to lifelong learning.

Chapter 3

Enhancing Social and Emotional Competencies

IT is outdoor playtime and 20 children are playing on the school playground. One head teacher and two assistants are walking around, watching the children, and making sure they are playing safely. As I approached the head teacher, two girls came sobbing incoherently toward her, one of them burying her head into the teacher's skirt. I thought one of them had hurt the other—what could cause such tears? Because the child's face was buried in the teacher's skirt, I worried that the child had been hit in the face. The teacher remained calm. I stood by waiting to determine if I needed to go into emergency mode. The teacher said to the girls calmly, "If you can stop crying, you can tell me what happened, and I can help." Within seconds the crying stopped. No blood was apparent. One child said, "She said she's not my friend anymore!" No scratches, no marks, just bruised emotions.

Most parents want their children to make and have friends. Shortly after their children go to school, parents begin asking their child, "Who did you play with today?" "Who are your friends?" Often, as the director of a preschool, I have to calm the fears of parents whose children still do not talk about having close playmates after the first week of school. Friendships take time to develop. They also require social and communication skills, and personal attributes including compassion for others, patience, empathy, and sensitivity to the needs of others.

Many times I overhear preschool teachers call children to a group meeting by referring to all of the children as "friends." It is a mistake to assume as a parent that your child will be friendly with all of the other children in the preschool classroom. This generally is not the case. Children, like their parents, will choose to make friends with peers who have similar interests, are easy and fun to play with, and who are kind to them. They also will learn that they like some children better than others, echoing the way friendships are made in the adult world.

Even though all of the children will not be their friends, children must learn to live as a community of learners who respect each other. Studies show that the "quality of peer relationships in early childhood predicts later success in intellectual growth, self-esteem, mental health, and school performance" (Riley, San Juan, Klinkner, & Ramminger, 2008, p. 36). There is some truth to the words in Robert Fulghum's (1989) book *All I Really Need to Know I Learned in Kindergarten*. His list of what is important in life referred to social and emotional competencies such as share everything, play fair, don't hit people, say you're sorry when you hurt somebody, and don't take things that aren't yours.

Social competencies are like other skills; they need to be practiced within authentic contexts. Playing with others gives young children experiences taking turns, sharing materials, and working together for common purposes. According to the Center on the Social and Emotional Foundations for Early Learning

(CSEFEL; 2007), children with a strong foundation in emotional literacy tolerate frustration better, get into fewer fights, engage in less destructive behavior, are healthier, less lonely, less impulsive, more focused, and have greater academic achievement.

Positive social behaviors (prosocial behaviors) occur when children have a healthy emotional foundation. Obviously, when children are angry or frustrated, they are more likely to be aggressive than when they are happy and content. Therefore, enhancing your child's social and emotional competencies relies on paying attention to the emotional well-being of your child, teaching skills that enhance social competencies, and providing the environment that prevents the most challenging behaviors from occurring.

Healthy Emotional Foundations

The emotional well-being of a child starts from birth. Much research on attachment suggests

> children with secure attachments to one or more caregivers at twelve months of age are more compliant with adults as toddlers, get into fewer fights as preschoolers and grade-schoolers, and undergo greater intellectual development through the early childhood years. (Riley et al., 2008, p. 6)

Securely attached children fare better socially, as well as academically. The literature concludes, "They are more empathetic and make friends more easily. They are less likely to become bullies or victims of bullies" (Riley et al., 2008, p. 14). The research also supports that early relationships children have with their caregivers are models for their future relationships with teach-ers. Emotionally healthy children develop positive relationships with the adults around them. Forming healthy relationships with adults begins with parents.

One of the easiest ways to make children feel secure is to provide a predictable environment and routine. Children feel safe when they know what will happen next. They begin to feel insecure when they cannot predict what mood their parent or caregiver will be in, and when their interactions are stressed, hurried, or erratic. Parents contribute to their child's emotional well-being by providing a loving, calm, predictable home envi-ronment. That does not mean that parents should control their child's every movement or stray from a schedule. On the con-trary, it means that parents should focus on providing an envi-ronment that develops their children's self-confidence to make appropriate decisions and to function independently.

Building a Healthy Emotional Environment

Parents can start from their child's birth to build a strong emotional foundation. Naturally, the physical closeness of hold-ing, caressing, and nurturing the baby begins to build the bonds of a healthy relationship. As children mature, the goal is to give them that feeling of security beyond their parents' reach. Allowing children the freedom to explore their world with ever increasing steps away from their parents provides initial ways of building a child's self-confidence. Even a little chore, such as putting toys away at night, begins to build a child's confidence by giving her the satisfaction of knowing she can do things on her own.

A healthy emotional environment includes parents taking on the role of teaching their children about their feelings and guiding them toward appropriate and positive behaviors instead of disciplining and punishing them. Before young children have words to express their anger, they express it in less than ideal and appropriate ways. Giving children the vocabulary to express their feelings is the first step in helping children identify their emotions and control their behaviors when emotions overcome them. The Center on the Social and Emotional Foundations for Early Learning (http://www.vanderbilt.edu/csefel) is a national resource center funded by the Office of Head Start and the Child Bureau. Its mission is to disseminate research and evidence-based practices to early childhood programs across the country. The Center provides several examples of ways that parents can help children identify their feelings:

- Talk about feelings.
- Ask your children to tell you how they feel.
- Teach new emotion words (e.g., frustrated, confused, anxious, excited, worried).
- Talk about how characters in a book, video, or on television may feel.
- Reflect on situations and discuss feelings.
- Accept and support your child's expression of feelings.
- Use books and art activities to talk about emotions. (CSEFEL, 2007)

Be sure as the parent, that your role is that of the nurturer, the guide, and the facilitator, and not just the disciplinarian. When your children misbehave, there is generally a reason. As the adult, you must recognize that the behavior serves a purpose for the child, and your role is to help the child find alternative ways (and acceptable alternatives, at that) to be responsive to the purpose. Simply punishing a child for crying because he does not get what he wants does not teach him how to request what he wants. Using the framework of guidance in the preschool classroom,

> The teacher helps children learn from their mistakes rather than punishing them for the mistakes they make; empowers children to solve problems rather than punishing them for having problems they cannot solve; and helps children accept consequences, but consequences that teach and leave self-esteem intact rather than punish. (Gartrell, 2004, p. 21)

Similar to the role of the teacher, the parents' role is to guide their children into strengthening their control over their emotions and behaviors. One way to do this is to teach your children to use the appropriate words to express their emotions. Table 6 includes a list of words parents can encourage their children to use when they talk about their emotions.

Another way to guide your child's emotional and behavioral self-control is to maximize the times when your children have some choice in the world and the environment around them. For example, rather than have the child fuss over what he or she will wear each morning, have the child help you pick out the outfit, perhaps by giving the child a choice of two that are acceptable to you.

Food often is the source of tantrums and inappropriate behavior. Talk to your child about food, give choices when you can that are acceptable to you (peas or carrots, apples or bananas, and so forth) and engage your child in helping you to prepare the food. When the child has some ownership in making his snack, lunch, or dinner, he is more likely to want to eat it. Picking up and put-

Table 6
Words to Express Emotion

Feeling words that 3–5-year-olds who are developing language typically understand include the following list. Parents should encourage their children to use these words when describing their emotions.

Affectionate	Cooperative	Free	Interested	Sad	Thrilled
Agreeable	Creative	Friendly	Jealous	Safe	Tired
Angry	Cruel	Frustrated	Joyful	Satisfied	Troubled
Annoyed	Curious	Gentle	Lonely	Scared	Unafraid
Awful	Depressed	Excited	Lost	Sensitive	
Bored	Disappointed	Fantastic	Loved	Serious	
Brave	Disgusted	Generous	Mad	Shy	
Calm	Ecstatic	Glad	Nervous	Stressed	
Capable	Embarrassed	Gloomy	Overwhelmed	Strong	
Caring	Enjoying	Guilty	Peaceful	Sick	
Cheerful	Excited	Happy	Pleasant	Stubborn	
Clumsy	Fantastic	Ignored	Proud	Tense	
Confused	Fearful	Impatient	Relaxed	Terrific	
Comfortable	Fed-up	Important	Relieved	Thoughtful	

Note. From *Positive Solutions for Families* [CD], by the Center on the Social and Emotional Foundations for Early Learning, 2007, Urbana-Champaign: University of Illinois at Urbana-Champaign. Available at http://www.vanderbilt.edu/cfesel. Copyright © 2007 by Center on the Social and Emotional Foundations for Early Learning. Reprinted with permission.

ting away toys may be a nonnegotiable chore, but allowing the chore to be done before or after the nap may be negotiable.

Be sure there is something pleasurable for the child to do when the chore is over. That builds natural consequences for her actions. (When the toys are put away, she has time to engage in loving family time.) I still remember when my 4-year-old said,

"But mommy, I don't like *your* choices!" In that case, I implored my son to create some of his own choices, with the condition that they would be acceptable to me. Teaching your children to problem solve is paramount to building the strong emotional foundation that enhances successful social behaviors.

Promoting Successful Social Behaviors

The skills that help children develop friendships are positive social behaviors such as taking turns, sharing, giving a compliment, helping another child, and learning to work together for a common purpose (e.g., building a block tower). It is important for children to experience learning these skills in authentic ways. Although there are many great children's books that one can use to talk about emotions and social skills, children need opportunities to try their skills out. If children do not have siblings, parents may need to find opportunities outside of the home to bring children together. Initially, it is wise to have young children play with only one other child at a time in what we now commonly refer to as the *play date.*

Play dates are informal opportunities for children to be with others with similar interests, including slightly older or younger children. Children who are especially shy benefit from having a play date with only one other child so it is not as overwhelming as having to be with several children at a time. Play dates give young children opportunities to negotiate and compromise with other children, to come to consensus while playing, to interact nonverbally and verbally, and to show an interest in others.

If your child is having difficulty making friends in a daycare setting, inviting one of the children from the center helps to build bonds of friendship that can be carried over into the daycare setting. If your child is having a friend over for the first time, it might be wise to talk to your child about some options of activities that he or she might like to have for his friend. Make sure you have the materials that you need for those activities. You also might like to review the acceptable places for the type of play they will be doing—building blocks in the playroom, using crayons and markers on the kitchen table, and so forth. That way, you are explicit about the boundaries and expectations before the friend comes to your house, and your child will be able to share these activities with his friend without you having to tell the children too many "rules" at one time and interrupting their play.

When Conflicts Arise

It is perfectly normal for conflicts to arise when two or more children play together. These conflicts are opportunities for learning and should be handled that way by adults who help children resolve them. When conflicts arise, the first priority is safety. If any child is physically hurting another child, of course, remove him from the situation. But, if children are arguing, give them support and help them to find the right words to explain what they need.

A typical scenario for conflict to arise would be when two children build a block structure. They argue over which blocks to use, or more commonly, one takes a block from the other—the exact block that the first child wanted to use. Rather than stopping the play and sending them both to time out (a strategy that I will discuss in detail later), take a moment to ask them what they are trying to accomplish, and how might they do that with the blocks that they share together. Then tell them that you are there to help them solve the problem if they need you, however, if they do not solve the problem and return to playing nicely, then they will have to choose something else to do. You might be surprised at how quickly they make amends and continue playing with the blocks.

The strategy for helping children resolve their own conflicts involves wisely trained adults who sequentially do the following: use choice language, support children's needs by giving them the words to express themselves, and then tell them what the consequence will be if they do not resolve their conflict. The consequence should almost always follow naturally from the situation. If two children cannot share a tricycle, then they need to put the tricycle away. If children do not use the markers appropriately (drawing on the kitchen floor instead of paper), then markers get put away. It's not that you as an adult are taking them away just to take them away, but you are showing children the natural consequences of their choices. They will see that *they* have control of their actions and play when they see the natural consequences (not the punishments) of their acts.

And No Time Outs!

When adults use natural consequences and choice language to let their children know what will happen when they do certain behaviors, they do not need time outs. Here I radically differ from my colleagues who write about the use of time out as behavior intervention strategies.

I have several reasons why I am firmly against using the time out strategy. Most importantly, it seldom helps the child.

Time out gives the adult an opportunity to put the child somewhere so that the adult can calm down. It rarely calms the child immediately. Although time out is widely used, I am not alone in my aversion to the strategy. According to Clewett, as sited in Gartrell (2004), "The time-out chair usually embarrasses the child, seldom teaches a positive lesson, and is almost always punishment" (p. 29).

More often than not, time out puts the child and the adult in a situation where the child uses oppositional behavior—the adult wants the child to sit in a chair, and the child does not want to do that. Although in theory, time out should not do this, most often in practice, the adult and child battle it out until the child becomes compliant. There are times of course, when our children do need to calm down before we can talk with them. At these moments, tell them you will talk to them as soon as they calm down and give them a space that they can designate for times when they feel they need to have quiet time or time to themselves. Parents too may need to walk away until they calm down. Children should not see their parents lose their temper. It is not a good model for resolving conflicts or solving problems. In addition, time out does not work when the same child has to do it again and again and again. Obviously, if the child is still misbehaving, then time out is an unsuccessful strategy.

An adult who puts a child in a time out takes control of the child's behavior and implicitly suggests that the adult is in charge of deciding when the child can play or join the group again. We want to teach children that they are in charge of *their own* behaviors. We want to tell them that they can play with their friends as soon as they can play appropriately and that you are willing to help them get back into the play.

Most often when children have tantrums or lose emotional control they are having a problem that they cannot solve alone. They do not want to lose control of their emotions or actions, but it just happens. As adults, we need to take those opportunities to reassure children that there are positive ways out of difficult situations. We need to give them words, alternatives, better ways of coping, and better choices for the next time they find themselves in those situations. We cannot provide them this type of help and guidance if we continually punish them for their mistakes or misbehaviors.

I share one last vivid example. When my son was 4 years old, I taught across the hallway from his preschool classroom. Each day at noon, a babysitter picked him up and took him home. I had lunch at noon, and could often come out into the hallway to give him a kiss goodbye before he left with his babysitter. One day I waited in the hallway for his classroom door to open. All of the children were in a line and putting on their winter coats. At his previous preschool, my son had been taught to put his coat on the floor and swing it behind him to put on the sleeves correctly. Apparently, when he did this, his zipper hit someone behind him who immediately started crying. The teacher, who saw none of this, responded immediately to the crying child who said my son hit him with his coat. Immediately, he was put in time out. All of the children left the room for dismissal and there he sat, crying and crying for an offense he did not even know he committed. Because I was standing and waiting for him to leave, I witnessed the whole incident and explained later to the teacher (because my son never did know what happened—he was removed before the child could tell the teacher what happened) that it was an accident.

The point is that too often time out is used as an immediate form of punishment, before parents or teachers even know what happened. When the teacher put my son in time out, she assumed his guilt and humiliated him. It's too late to come back and figure out what happened; when the adult is in the role of punisher, it leaves little room to take on the role of a nurturing facilitator to help the child deal with social problems.

Teach Social Skills Explicitly

From the very beginning, talk to your child about positive behaviors that you would like to see and that you expect him or her to display. For example, before going to a friend's house you might have a conversation about what your child and the friend might do. You should use words that describe prosocial behaviors such as, "You and John might share a snack, build sandcastles, or play a game together." If your child is crying because he's sad, you might help him identify that feeling by saying, "I'm sorry that you are sad. How can I help you feel better?" or, better still, "What can *you do* to feel better?"

Transitions are especially hard times for young children. If they are playing with friends and want to stay longer, but you are in a hurry, acknowledge that you understand that they might like to stay and play, but that you are in a hurry and could arrange for another visit again. Sometimes children just need to be reassured that their fun times will happen again when they are quickly whisked away from a situation in which they were enjoying themselves.

In addition to acknowledging your children's feelings, parents should be sensitive to and praise successes—when their children act appropriately (take a turn, help another child, show empathy). For example, tell them, "I noticed that you helped Jamie find her shoe. That was so nice of you to take the time to help her." When your child calms down immediately after you say, "I can talk to you as soon as you stop crying," tell her, "I'm so glad you stopped crying so that we can talk." Use praise specifically for the behaviors that you want to encourage. Do not say, "You're a good girl (or bad girl)," depending on the behavior.

When the child makes a mistake, acknowledge that it was a poor decision and that it has consequences, but give her the language and the alternative to help her the next time the same situation happens. Although I grew up with the mantra, "Two wrongs don't make a right," if your child hits another child back, it is more appropriate to say, "It was not appropriate that Jill hit you, but you may not hit or hurt any child. The next time someone hits you, tell an adult." The difference between telling a child, "Two wrongs don't make a right," and "tell an adult," is that you are offering your child an alternative and teaching her to solve problems. Sometimes those problems need an adult's intervention.

The adult can help children to see things from others' perspectives. Leaving their egocentric world does not happen all in one day. Children gradually mature from seeing their own view of the world, to recognizing that others may see things differently. There are many great children's books that lend themselves to teaching children about how others might be feeling and thinking. When reading the book, you might ask how a character is feeling, or how it would make you feel if the same thing happened to you or your sister or brother. I have included a list of books compiled by the Center on the Social Emotional Foundations for Early Learning as Table 7.

Using puppets is another way to engage children in talking about feelings or incidents that happened to them. "Sesame

Table 7
Children's Books That Focus on Emotions

ABC Look at Me!: A Lift-and-Learn Book by Roberta Grobel Intrater

Amazing Grace by Mary Hoffman

And Here's to You by David Elliott

Andrew's Angry Words by Dorothea Lachner

Big Al by Andrew Clements

Can You Tell How Someone Feels? by Nita Everly

Can You Use a Good Voice? by Nita Everly

Care Bears: The Day Nobody Shared by Nancy Parent

The Chocolate Covered Cookie Tantrum by Deborah Blumenthal

Chrysanthemum by Kevin Henkes

Don't Forget I Love You by Miriam Moss

Double-Dip Feelings by Barbara Cain

The Feel Good Book by Todd Parr

The Feelings Book by Todd Parr

Fox Makes Friends by Adam Relf

Franklin's Bad Day by Paulette Bourgeois & Brenda Clark

Franklin in the Dark by Paulette Bourgeois & Brenda Clark

Franklin's New Friend by Paulette Bourgeois & Brenda Clark

The Grouchy Ladybug by Eric Carle

Hands Are Not for Hitting by Martine Agassi

Happy and Sad, Grouchy and Glad by Constance Allen

Heartprints by P. K. Hallinan

How Are You Peeling?: Food With Moods by Saxton Freymann & Joost Elffers

How Do I Feel? ¿Cómo me siento? by Houghton Mifflin

How I Feel Frustrated by Marcia Leonard

How to be a Friend: A Guide to Making Friends and Keeping Them by Laurie Krasny Brown & Marc Brown

Hunter's Best Friend at School by Laura Malone Elliott

Hurty Feelings by Helen Lester

I Am Not Going to School Today! by Robie H. Harris

I'm Sorry by Sam McBratney

I Can Do It Myself by Emily Perl Kingsley

If You're Happy and You Know It! by Jane Cabrera

It's Hard to Share My Teacher by Joan Singleton Prestine

The Kissing Hand by Audrey Penn

Lilly's Purple Plastic Purse by Kevin Henkes

The Little Engine That Could by Watty Piper

The Little Mouse, the Red Ripe Strawberry, and the Big Hungry Bear by
    Don & Audry Wood

Little Teddy Bear's Happy Face Sad Face by Lynn Offerman

Lizzy's Ups and Downs by Jessica Harper

Making Friends by Fred Rogers

Making Friends by Janine Amos

Margaret and Margarita/Margarita y Margaret by Lynn Reiser

Matthew and Tilly by Rebecca C. Jones

My Friend and I by Lisa Jahn-Clough

My Many Colored Days by Dr. Seuss

No Such Thing by Jackie French Koller

On Monday When It Rained by Cherryl Kachenmeister

One Lonely Sea Horse by Saxton Freymann & Joost Elffers

Perro Grande. . . Perro Pequeño/Big Dog. . . Little Dog by P. D. Eastman

Proud of Our Feelings by Lindsay Leghorn

The Rainbow Fish by Marcus Pfister

Sam's First Day/Sam y su primer dia de escuela by David Mills & Lizzie
    Finlay

See How I Feel by Julie Aigner-Clark

Share and Take Turns by Cheri J. Meiners

Simon and Molly Plus Hester by Lisa Jahn-Clough

Smudge's Grumpy Day by Miriam Moss

Sometimes I'm Bombaloo by Rachel Vail

Sometimes I Feel Awful by Joan Singleton Prestine

Sometimes I Feel Like a Storm Cloud by Lezlie Evans

Sometimes I Share by Carol Nicklaus

Sunshine & Storm by Elisabeth Jones & James Coplestone

Susan Laughs by Jeanne Willis

Talk and Work It Out by Cheri J. Meiners

That Makes Me Mad! by Steven Kroll

That's What a Friend Is by P. K. Hallinan

The Three Grumpies by Tamra Wight

Today I Feel Silly and Other Moods That Make My Day by Jamie Lee Curtis

Too Loud Lilly by Sophie Laguna

Try and Stick With It by Cheri J. Meiners

26 Big Things Small Hands Do by Coleen Paratore

The Very Clumsy Click Beetle by Eric Carle

The Very Lonely Firefly by Eric Carle

The Way I Feel by Janan Cain

We Are Best Friends by Aliki

Wemberly Worried by Kevin Henkes

What Makes Me Happy? by Catherine & Laurence Anholt

When I Am / Cuando Estoy by Gladys Rosa-Mendoza

When I Feel Angry by Cornelia Maude Spelman

When I'm Angry: A Language of Parenting Guide by Jane Aaron

When Sophie Gets Angry–Really, Really Angry . . . by Molly Bang

Whistle for Willie / Sílbale a Willie by Ezra Jack Keats

Words Are Not for Hurting by Elizabeth Verdick

You're All My Favorites by Sam McBratney

You Can Do It, Sam by Amy Hest

Note. From *Positive Solutions for Families* [CD], by the Center on the Social and Emotional Foundations for Early Learning (2007), Urbana-Champaign: University of Illinois at Urbana-Champaign. Available at http://www.vanderbilt.edu/cfesel. Copyright © 2007 by Center on the Social and Emotional Foundations for Early Learning. Reprinted with permission.

Street" characters have taught children explicitly about emotions, feelings, and ways to solve friendship problems for years. Parents, too, can create what's commonly called *social stories* to enact a scenario with puppets that teaches specific feelings and ways to approach social situations. Puppets also introduce a sense of creativity and provide a great home activity—let your child help you make homemade puppets from socks or paper bags. Allow her to name her puppet, and give yours a name too. Creating a sense of character your child can relate to will only help cement the social behaviors you have those puppets teach later.

Bullies

Be on the lookout for bullies and bullying. Bullying is social behavior "gone wrong." Teasing is common in almost any group of children, but beware of children who intentionally make repeated efforts to hurt your child either verbally or physically. As we know, not all parents or homes can provide the safe, warm, and secure trusting environment that lead to positive social behaviors. Your child may be a victim of a bully or may even try to bully others. Bullies tend to pick on the most vulnerable children. Girls may say things like, "I won't be your friend anymore," or worse, give another child the "silent treatment." Boys may tease a more vulnerable peer or be more physical with other children. Remember too that bullies come in every shape, size, gender, and race. Try not to stereotype the biggest kid in your child's class as a sure bully; it could just as easily be a smaller child who exhibits bullying behaviors.

Help your children recognize signs of bullying and talk explicitly about not playing with the child who bullies, or give your children words to stand up for themselves. Role-play scenarios where your children can learn to stand up to bullies. Bullying behavior can be verbal, psychological, or physical. If your child shows signs of anxiousness around certain children, talk to your child and find out why he or she might not like to play with a particular child. Help your child get away from the bullying behavior by giving your child strategies for finding new friends. By all means, teach your child to report threatening behavior to an adult. If you feel that this behavior is happening in your child's daycare or preschool situation, report it immediately to the teacher. Children who bully other children need help. They need to find other ways to feel powerful, self-confident, and self-worth other than exerting power over their peers.

What do you do if you find out your child is the bully? If your child is bullying another child, find out why he or she may be victimizing other children. Talk to your child. Role-play scenarios where your child has to take another child's point of view. Discuss with your child the feelings of others. Children who bully others often were bullied by someone else first. Make sure your child feels respected and is treated with compassion. Give your child unconditional love, and make sure you are building his or her self-esteem. Help your child feel positive about him- or herself.

Remember children often do what is modeled for them. Be a good role model by being empathetic and compassionate toward others. Offer specific praise to your child for being kind and playing appropriately with friends. Provide natural consequences when your child is unkind toward others. If your child consistently bullies one child, then make sure he does not have the opportunity to play with that child until the behavior changes. Do not be afraid to seek professional help for you and your child if you continue to witness bullying behavior. There may be some deep-rooted issues that manifest aggressive, bullying behavior in your child. Although you may do your best to stop the behavior, you may need help addressing the underlying reasons for such behavior.

Challenging Behaviors

All behavior serves a purpose. Children act certain ways because it benefits them. Challenging behaviors generally refer to aggressive or other forms of inappropriate behavior that are the most difficult to change or extinguish. Some common challenging behaviors of children in this age group include tantrums, hitting other children, or disrupting the play and learning of others with their voices or demands for attention. For the teacher, students who have short attention spans also can be challenging. These are the children who have trouble sitting in a large-group meeting. They tend to want to walk around or put their hands on the child next to them because they really cannot focus on what the teacher is doing with the rest of the children.

Challenging behaviors interfere with learning and positive social interactions. It is believed that challenging behaviors are indicators or predictors of more serious problems to come later in the child's life, including substance abuse, delinquency, or antisocial behavior. Challenging behaviors also are linked to children with other risk factors such as poverty, single parent homes, or negative parenting practices. Most importantly, children with challenging behaviors frequently experience rejection from their peers.

Parents and teachers alike must work with children with challenging behaviors systematically. The goal is not to "control the child," but to provide support to enable the child to work through problems and to solve social conflicts without tension, stress, or aggression.

One strategy parents can try is to develop a self-monitoring system that helps their children be aware, be responsible, and take control of their own behaviors. A self-monitoring system might be a clipboard with a desired behavior written on it so that the child will know what is expected. The child can draw a picture of the desired behavior and use it as an icon to put on the chart. Every time the child does the desired behavior, then the child can put a tally mark on the clipboard. Be sure to target positive behaviors! The desired behavior should be observable so that there will be no question in the child's mind if he did the behavior or not. For example, perhaps the goal is for the child to say a kind word to a peer. An icon for a kind word is put on the sheet of paper attached to a clipboard. Every time the child says a kind word, he marks a tally on his clipboard.

Some parents use extrinsic rewards to go along with the tally marks. For example, if the child says five nice things to one peer, the peer can come home with him for a play date. I would advise parents to use natural consequences instead of using bribes or extrinsic rewards. Giving your child praise and attention for doing the right thing may be sufficient. If you feel the child needs stickers or happy faces, or "extra time" doing something he loves, then by all means use whatever motivational strategy works for the child to gain confidence in himself to control his own behavior. The purpose of self-monitoring is to empower the child to take control of his or her actions. What you do not want to have happen is for you as the parent to threaten the child with the tally marks on the clipboard. For example, do not say, "If you throw the block, you will not get a tally mark." Then you would be right back to the pattern of exerting external control.

You also do not want your child to feel a reliance on extrinsic rewards. What you would like to have happen naturally is for your child to grow stronger friendships by being kinder to and less aggressive with other children.

Children with severe behavior problems may need a more intensive approach called *applied behavior analysis* (ABA). This method, scientifically based on the behaviorist tradition, uses what we know about behavior and applies it to young children to bring about changes in their behavior. The first step is to examine the environmental components that precede the challenging behavior and systematically plan to change one component at a time so that the child does not engage in any inappropriate behavior.

Children with disabilities, or those who have difficulty communicating their needs, are typically given behavior plans with applied behavior analysis. Specific behaviors are targeted to improve. Rather than a self-monitoring system, the parent or teacher would plan an intervention and collect data as an experimental scientist would do, to determine the effectiveness of the intervention. In some instances, the intervention could be a self-monitoring plan.

The basic principles underlying applied behavior analysis is that one tries to extinguish negative behaviors by punishing them or ignoring them and one tries to increase appropriate behaviors by praising and rewarding those behaviors. Applied behavior analysis is becoming a popular intervention for children with autism and other communication disorders. For more information about applied behavior analysis, parents may want to check out the Web sites for the Institute for Applied Behavior Analysis (http://www.iaba.com) or the Association for Applied Behavior Analysis International (http://www.abainternational.org).

Challenging behaviors can crop up at any point in a child's life. Right now, you may be worried about stopping your child from hitting another so he will not be ostracized at school or thrown out of a private daycare setting. When your child becomes a teenager, he may exhibit other, often more dangerous, forms of challenging behaviors.

Challenging behaviors can be improved with supports and a behavior plan in place. To extinguish challenging behaviors, parents need to make sure those behaviors are not rewarded, even unintentionally. For example, if your child is constantly picking on his or her younger sibling and if every time that happens, you stop to talk to your child, then in fact, your child is getting what he wants—attention. Tell your child you are happy to read or play with him as long as he does not bother his younger sibling. Be consistent. Consistency is paramount to changing a behavior.

Conclusion

The ABCs of Guiding the Child (Dreikurs & Goldman, 1990) summarizes general principles of parenting, provides a basic understanding of reasons for misbehavior, and gives practical suggestions for encouraging your child to develop positively both socially and emotionally. The authors promote parent respect for the child. They state, "Parents who show respect for the child— while winning his respect for them—teach the child to respect himself and others" (p. 2). They also reiterate the need for children to feel secure,

A child to feel secure, needs:

Courage—"I'm willing to take a chance"
Confidence—"I'll be able to handle it"
Optimism—"Things will turn out all right." (Dreikurs &
Goldman, 1990, p. 6)

Parents have the ultimate responsibility for putting their children on the right path to developing healthy friendships. As parents, you must provide your children with safe environments that model caring relationships. Keep in mind you will need to:

1. Provide opportunities for your children to play with others.
2. Give children the language they need to identify and express their feelings.
3. Accept the role of the facilitator when children need your help solving problems.
4. Support your child's ownership and control of his or her own behaviors by providing natural consequences for his or her actions and choices.
5. Teach explicitly the skills of taking turns, sharing, helping, and caring for others.

Of course there will be times when children make mistakes or lose control of their emotions. There will be times when your child says an unkind comment that is overheard. We all have been embarrassed by our children's poor social skills. However, children's social skills will mature along with their cognitive and academic skills. A checklist for monitoring your child's social skills is included in Table 8. When children learn to express their emotions in writing, they will have additional avenues to share their feelings and communicate with you and their friends.

Table 8

The Social Attributes Checklist
(McClellan & Katz, 2001, p. 2)

I. Individual Attributes

The child:

- ❏ Is usually in a positive mood.
- ❏ Is not excessively dependent on adults.
- ❏ Usually comes to the program willingly.
- ❏ Usually copes with rebuffs adequately.
- ❏ Shows the capacity to empathize.
- ❏ Has positive relationships with one or two peers; shows the capacity to really care about them and miss them if they are absent.
- ❏ Displays the capacity for humor.
- ❏ Does not seem to be acutely lonely.

II. Social Skills Attributes

The child usually:

- ❏ Approaches others positively.
- ❏ Expresses wishes and preferences clearly; gives reasons for actions and positions.
- ❏ Asserts own rights and needs appropriately.
- ❏ Is not easily intimidated by bullies.
- ❏ Expresses frustrations and anger effectively and without escalating disagreements or harming others.
- ❏ Gains access to ongoing groups at play and work.
- ❏ Enters ongoing discussion on the subject; makes relevant contributions to ongoing activities.
- ❏ Takes turns fairly easily.

❑ Shows interest in others; exchanges information with and requests information from others appropriately.

❑ Negotiates and compromises with others appropriately.

❑ Does not draw inappropriate attention to self.

❑ Accepts and enjoys peers and adults of ethnic groups other than his or her own.

❑ Interacts nonverbally with other children with smiles, waves, nods, etc.

III. Peer Relationship Attributes

The child:

❑ Is usually accepted versus neglected or rejected by other children.

❑ Is sometimes invited by other children to join them in play, friendship, and work.

❑ Is named by other children as someone they are friends with or like to play and work with.

Helping children to communicate their feelings, thoughts, and ideas is paramount to helping them develop friendships and getting along with peers. Even in our adult lives, communication is the key to getting along with our spouses, colleagues, and children. We must remember the complexities of interactions, and be patient as our young children develop the communication skills that will enhance their relationships with others.

Chapter 4

Choosing a Preschool for Your Child

DREW, a 4-year-old, whimpered as he had to get into his mother's car. He folded his hands when the car stopped in front of his preschool and refused to get out of his booster seat, which by now was unlocked by his frantic mother trying to get to work. His mother tried to persuade him, offering him candy when he gets home. He still refused to get out of the car. She picked him up and carried him crying (and heavy) into his classroom, making an excuse to his teacher that he had a bad morning that day. Unfortunately, every morning was a bad morning for Drew because he dreaded preschool. He was often in "time out," fearful of letters home between the teacher and his mother, and generally unhappy at school because he could not sit still and listen during calendar time. He wasn't interested in playing with magnetic alphabet letters or coloring the picture of an object that matched the letter of the week. Clearly, this preschool was not the best "fit" for Drew or perhaps any other active 4-year-old boy. But, how do parents know what preschool will be best for their child?

According to a 2002 U.S. Census Bureau report, 11.6 million of the 18.5 million children from birth through age 5 counted in the 2000 census were in some form of regular childcare arrangement. Of that data, the Census Bureau found that 6.4 million of those children were in nonrelative care, with 4.1 of those children being in a specific, organized care facility (U.S. Census Bureau, 2002). Certainly, it is important to determine the quality of early education programs and to examine the basis for how parents make decisions about childcare or preschool placements. In other words, what should parents look for when they have to choose a preschool or childcare environment for their child?

Patten and Ricks (2000) in their review of the research on childcare quality stated, "Defining high quality child care is difficult, however; there is general agreement that the development of children should be enhanced rather than put at risk by their out-of-home care experiences" (p. 1). Researchers studying the quality of care delineate structural and process features. Process features include how staff respond to children, the way teachers talk with children, how staff approach discipline, and appropriateness of learning activities. Structural features include group size, child-adult ratio, level of staff education/training, staff turnover rate, quality/quantity of space, and quality/quantity of materials.

These features are some of the same indicators of quality that are found in the National Association for the Education of Young Children (NAEYC) accreditation standards. Parents who move to a new community may search the NAEYC Web site and find accredited programs in their area. To be accredited, early childhood programs must adhere to the defined criteria for each of the following 10 standards. The standards are explained in

detail on NAEYC's Web site, available at http://www.naeyc.org/
academy/standards. The standards consist of:

1. Relationships
2. Curriculum
3. Teaching
4. Assessment of Child Progress
5. Health
6. Teachers
7. Families
8. Community Relationships
9. Physical Environment
10. Leadership and Management (NAEYC, n.d.b).

Articulated under each standard are observable policies or
practices that should be followed by accredited programs. Under
the first standard, for example, the goal is to have positive relationships between families and center staff, between children and
their caregivers or preschool teachers. To build these positive relationships, parents may expect to see ongoing communications
(newsletters, notes home, and so forth) and a parent handbook
that explains school policies and procedures (NAEYC, n.d.b).

There are many criteria listed under the standard of curriculum, with one of the most comprehensive ones stating,

The curriculum guides teachers to incorporate content,
concepts, and activities that foster social, emotional,
physical, language, and cognitive development and that
integrate key areas of content including literacy, mathematics, science, technology, creative expression and the
arts, health and safety, and social studies. (NAEYC, n.d.c,
¶ 11)

Under the curriculum standard, other measures of high quality include providing ongoing assessment to guide and individualize instruction, using appropriate materials, and employing a schedule that allows students to engage in activities over long periods of time in a variety of organizational groupings (small group, large group, individual). Thus, the schedule is an important artifact to examine when visiting and evaluating a particular program. The use and types of materials also are indicative of how children will be engaged. According to NAEYC (n.d.c), materials and equipment used to implement the curriculum:

- reflect the lives of the children and families;
- reflect the diversity found in society, including gender, age, language, and abilities;
- provide for children's safety while being appropriately challenging;
- encourage exploration, experimentation, and discovery;
- promote action and interaction;
- are organized to support independent use;
- are rotated to reflect changing curriculum and accommodate new interests and skill levels;
- are rich in variety; and
- accommodate children's special needs. (NAEYC, n.d.c, ¶ 11)

The NAEYC accreditation criteria also reflect the importance of having trained and educated staff, as well as qualified directors or managers of preschool programs. Many of their standards reflect the importance of the structural features of the businesses or schools that house our children. They give optimal child/staff ratios to prevent the pitfalls of overcrowding. If early childhood programs have appropriate teacher to student ratios, then it follows that the interactions between staff and children could be more frequent and hopefully, more meaningful (talking with students about their work, not just about rules, procedures, and following directions). Typically, for a classroom of 3- and 4-year-old children, it is ideal to have one teacher per 10 students.

To most parents, though, the most important factors for choosing a setting for their children are related to the relationships that staff members have with the children, and the type of things that their children will actually do once they get there. Leaders in the field of early childhood education insist that young children are capable of learning about the world around them in authentic and meaningful ways.

Finding the Right Fit for Your Child

What exactly should parents do to find the best preschool for their child? Their first steps might include:

1. Search the Internet for NAEYC accredited programs because some measure of quality is already inherent in the accreditation.
2. Find out more about local programs through word of mouth. Where are your friends and neighbors sending their children?
3. Set up an appointment to talk with the administrator of the program. Questions to ask the administrator might include:
   a. How are the teachers certified?
   b. What type of professional development does the administrator build in to his or her calendar or the teachers' schedule?

    c.   What policies are in place for when children are sick or hurt?

    d.   What type of curriculum do the teachers follow?

    e.   How do the teachers monitor progress?

    f.   How do teachers involve parents?

    g.   How do teachers communicate to parents?

    h.   What is highly valued in the program?

    i.   What type of food service do they have, if any? How is food monitored? (Regular checks by health department?)

    j.   What should parents expect to see in the classroom?

    k.   Is there any type of advisory board or council to the program?

4.   Make an appointment to observe the program.

In Katz's (2007) article entitled, "What to Look for When Visiting Early Childhood Classes," she defines quality preschool settings by examining five underlying principles that must be evident for the environment to provide optimal learning for young children:

1. Strengthen children's understanding of their own experience.
2. The younger the children, the more they learn from direct firsthand experience.
3. The younger the children, the more they learn through interactive rather than passive processes.
4. The younger the children, the more important it is that what they are learning has horizontal versus vertical relevance.
5. Children's dispositions to seek in-depth understanding of experience and events is strengthened when they have early experience of in-depth investigations. (pp. 35–36)

What are the tell-tale signs in the early childhood classrooms that teachers are attending to these principles? What are the quality indicators that the teachers or daycare providers have taken these principles into account? Parents also must be careful observers because what is intended to occur might not actually be happening. The following list includes observable indicators of best practices that when visible are likely to find children in a warm, caring, healthy environment where they will become engaged in investigating the world around them.

Observable Indicators of Quality

Observable Indicator 1: Teachers Talking to and With Children Physically at Their Level

If you only see teachers standing tall, giving directions, directing traffic as children go back and forth, beware! The most important indicator of quality is positive relationships. Teachers need to be engaged with children, talking to them about what they are doing, and what they would like to do. They need to be probing students' with questions that require students to give their ideas, their opinions, or their understandings of a particular topic. They need to engage the children in higher level thinking and problem-solving processes. Teachers should be talking quietly with individuals or small groups of children most of the time. For large-group instruction, teachers should hold students' attention by engaging them in large-group activities and not by shouts or threats to listen.

Observable Indicator 2: Children Talking, Playing, and Working With Other Children

If students are silently ushered in and out of a room, directed to do whole-group tasks where they cannot talk with each other, again, be wary. For children to build positive relationships and learn to enhance their own social competencies, they need opportunities to work collaboratively, to listen to other children's ideas, and to negotiate their position when conflicts arise. As discussed in the previous chapter, incorporating many opportunities for children to work on common and shared goals builds friendships and self-competence.

Observable Indicator 3: Warm and Aesthetically Pleasing Physical Environment

Much like I proposed for your child's private spaces at home, the ideal early childhood classroom also is inviting. It should not be cluttered. A calming environment generally has neutral or muted tones. Attention to natural colors and textures facilitates students' understanding of the nature around them. Sorting of markers and paper by colors or hues inherently teaches children about the color spectrum and the pleasing ways that colors can be combined and contrasted.

Observable Indicator 4: Evidence of Meaningful Work—Documentation

If you walk into a classroom and see 20 jack-o-lanterns posted on a bulletin board in October, large Disney characters all over the walls and ceilings, or worksheets demonstrating that a child can write his or her name five times, you're not seeing a classroom that displays *meaningful* work. The classroom walls and surfaces should be clean and organized, but also tastefully display *what is highly valued* in the classroom: children's work and experiences. There is a growing literature on the role that documentation plays in children's learning (see, for example, Helm, Beneke, & Steinheimer, 2007; Reggio Children & Project Zero, 2001). The learning processes are carefully documented with conversation and displayed on documentation boards to inform and engage others who visit the school about the children's experiences. Extensive use of digital photography to display photographs of children in the process of collaborating, problem solving, observing, asking questions, and representing their ideas is a sign that the teachers value children's input and ideas.

Observable Indicator 5: Appropriate Materials Where Children Can Access Them

In Reggio Emilia, the materials given to children are the languages that they use to express their ideas. Educators in Reggio confirm this idea:

> Our environments are like landscapes of possibilities and suggestions. . . . If we value the children's desire and pleasure in carrying out investigations, either by themselves or in groups, then we must make sure that the sort of materials we provide allow this to happen. (Reggio Children & Project Zero, 2001, p. 67)

Materials provide contexts for creativity, interaction, and collaborative work. Items such as puppets, wooden building blocks, transparent and translucent objects to explore on the light table, pattern blocks, bound blank booklets of all shapes and sizes, and art materials such as multicultural paints, crayons, markers, fabric, wire, yarn, string, construction paper, and recyclable materials

Figure 2. A collection of materials for use by young children at a Reggio Emilia school.

should be accessible and organized for children to use (see Figure 2 for a picture of assorted materials available for student use at a Reggio Emilia school). In her description of the materials that she saw in Reggio Emilia, Kang (2007) described how the materials facilitated students' creativity and expression of ideas.

> In one of the Balducci preschool classrooms, a girl and a boy created a flower garden on the light table. Dried flowers, leaves, and rhinestones became a beautiful bunch of flowers, wrinkled green paper became the grass around the flowers, and a cluster of sliced green plastic became a bush. The children turned colorful candy wrappers into another bouquet of flowers. The light table added more aesthetic ambience to the garden. (p. 47)

Beware of the classroom environment where materials and displays do not change throughout the year. The materials should be fluid and changing with the interests of the children or projects that are undertaken. Look for the environment that captures the interest of the children, as well as the adults, in the room.

Observable Indicator 6: Evidence of a Literacy-Rich Environment

A literacy-rich environment has enticing books displayed in areas throughout the room, a well-organized library with books categorized for children to understand (books about animals, books about weather, poetry, and so on), different levels of books from picture books to chapter books, and most importantly, evidence that children are agents of print! If all you see is word walls, the alphabet, and numbers throughout the room, the focus of literacy is not on meaning. If you see lists of ideas that children have generated, vocabulary lists that have been derived from topics the children are studying, or stories that have been dictated by individuals or groups of students, you know that the children have been engaged in discussion and have had opportunities to associate print and text with their own words and ideas. A literacy-rich environment is one where children have opportunities to speak, listen, read, and write frequently. There should be much evidence in the room of these activities.

Observable Indicator 7: Evidence of Creative and Critical Thinking

Students' self-expression and representations of their thinking processes should be evident in the classroom. Examples of children brainstorming, categorizing ideas, sorting, synthesizing, and evaluating information should be obvious to observers. Students should be highly motivated to learn and the classroom environment should not rely on management systems that overemphasize extrinsic reward systems. As Hennessey (2005) stated, "Intrinsic motivation is conducive to creativity, and extrinsic motivation is usually detrimental" (p. 4). Furthermore, she noted,

> Whether the targets of an investigation are preschoolers, fifth graders, or college students, the findings are consistent. Over the years, five environmental constraints have consistently proven to be sure-fire killers of intrinsic motivation and creativity: (a) expected reward (b) expected evaluation (c) competition (d) surveillance and (e) time limits. (p. 5)

Although these factors are common in many public school classrooms, teachers can tamper them by preserving students' sense of self-determination. In situations where students feel in control of their own destiny, motivation and creativity may not suffer. Early childhood environments should include elements of choice in nearly every aspect of the curriculum and not have an overemphasis on external rewards for good behavior or good work. Children should not be comparing their work to others. Instead, they should be learning cooperative and collaborative ways to help each other learn.

Implementation of Best Practices

There are many ways to implement best practices in early childhood education. But, nearly all the literature on best practices reflect Katz's (1995) belief that the younger the children, the more active they should be in their own learning. She advocates involving students in project investigations, which will be discussed in detail along with other program models below, and finally, she asks questions that are indicators of quality from the students' perspectives:

1. Do I usually feel welcome rather than captured?
2. Do I usually feel that I am someone who belongs rather than someone who is just part of the crowd?
3. Do I usually feel accepted, understood, and protected by the adults rather than scolded or neglected by them?
4. Am I usually accepted by some of my peers rather than isolated or rejected by them?
5. Am I usually addressed seriously and respectfully, rather than as someone who is "precious" or "cute"?
6. Do I find most of the activities engaging, absorbing, and challenging, rather than just amusing, fun, entertaining, or exciting?
7. Do I find most of the experiences interesting, rather than frivolous or boring?
8. Do I find most of the activities meaningful, rather than frustrating or confusing?
9. Am I usually glad to be here, rather than reluctant to come, and eager to leave? (Katz, 1995, p. 122)

If the answer is positive to these questions, then parents can rest assured that their children are having mostly happy and positive educational experiences in their early childhood setting.

Making a Good Match

How do you know if the program is a good match for your child? It is probably easier to describe symptoms you might see when a program is *not* a good match for your child, than to describe the signs of a good match. When a child is happy at pre-school and learning in a joy-filled environment, chances are the child will act like he typically does. It's when there is a mismatch that a child will begin to show signs of stress, unhappiness, or uneasiness with his daily routine that includes preschool.

For example, if your 3-year-old who has not needed diapers in more than 6 months begins to wet her bed, then something could be wrong (either physically or mentally). Regression or clinginess to a parent is one of the first signs that children use to demonstrate their stress. If your child starts to use more aggressive behavior (my son started biting) than he usually does, then that could be a sign that there is something troubling or frustrating him. If your child simply cries and does not want to go to school—consider taking a closer look at your child's classroom. Spend some time observing your child in the classroom. See if she is really happy while she is at school. Sometimes, the symptoms parents see at home are because their children have held up so well during the day. They are fatigued when they get home and they can't have the same level of self-control at home as they did in school.

Sometimes a preschool may be making your child happy, but you may not be satisfied. I often hear parents say they think their children could learn more than what is offered in their child's preschool setting. Parents may be frustrated with the lack of intellectual engagement their children have in certain preschool activities. Although their children are perfectly happy playing all morning, (and much can be learned through play), parents may want some time for more literacy activities, more opportunities to have children engaged in problem solving, or choices that tap into students' mathematical or scientific inclinations and curiosities. That is why it is so important that parents become knowledgeable about the curricular and philosophical approaches that guide their children's preschool activities. There can be many different types of programs that offer high-quality early education experiences. In the next section, I will discuss the wide variety of preschool settings that can be found, and some of the common curricular approaches parents might see when they observe the programs.

Types of Programs and Curricular Approaches

Preschool settings are among the most varied of all educational environments. Children can go to preschool in churches, in home daycare, or in center-based programs. Preschools can be private, parochial, or federally mandated. Some preschools are in laboratory settings and are found on 2- or 4-year college campuses throughout the country. Some preschool programs are part of vocational programs in high schools.

In the United States, children with disabilities have a legal right to start a free and appropriate education at age 3 and public school systems must have early childhood programs to educate them. Head Start programs are federally funded programs for children ages 3–5 from families with income below the federal poverty levels. In addition, children whose families receive public assistance or foster children are also eligible. Head Start programs also may enroll up to 10% of their student population who do not meet the income level or other criteria. The next few sections will discuss the various types of preschool settings beyond the traditional prekindergarten program offered by local public schools based on the curricular approaches each setting encourages.

Curricular approaches are almost as varied as the programs themselves. For example, in private faith-based programs, the curriculum generally includes prayer, Bible stories, and religious songs. In Head Start programs, curriculum often is mandated so that different centers follow similar procedures for licensing, reporting, assessing, and providing services to families. Becoming familiar with different curricular approaches will help you know what types of things to look for when you visit a preschool and give you a better understanding of the differences that can occur between different schools.

The Project Approach

I chose to talk about the Project Approach first because it is the approach I know best. Long before I studied early childhood education, I received my degree in gifted education. Project-based or inquiry-based learning often is incorporated into programs for gifted students because it challenges the students and affords them opportunities to seek more in-depth knowledge in their interest areas. As the Director of University Primary School at the University of Illinois at Urbana-Champaign for the past 12 years, I have had the good fortune to work with Professor Lilian Katz, one of the most well-known early childhood educators both in the United States and abroad. She and her colleague Sylvia Chard wrote the book *Engaging Children's Minds* (Katz & Chard, 2000) that articulated the investigative curricular approach for young children called the Project Approach.

According to Katz and Chard (2000),

A project is a piece of research abut a topic—one that may be related to a larger theme—in which children's ideas, questions, theories, predictions, and interests are major determinants of the experiences provided and the work accomplished. (p. 5)

By using the Project Approach, teachers may be responsive to children's interests. In contrast to theme-based curricular units, students are involved in the development of the study and the curriculum emerges in investigations based on students' questions and interests. Themes and units, on the other hand, are generally a set of activities planned and organized by the teacher around a specific topic that the teacher has chosen like fall, space, gardens, and so forth. Several examples of project investigations may be viewed on the University Primary School Web site: http://www.ed.uiuc.edu/ups/projects.

In classrooms where the Project Approach is implemented, parents may expect to see evidence of students' firsthand investigations. They would see students collecting data by using questionnaires, interviewing experts, making observational drawings, and designing experiments to test their predictions and hypotheses. They also would see students representing their data and findings with bar graphs, charts, 3-dimensional models, drawings, books, and displays. The children would be actively working together on a topic that is interesting to them and the teacher would facilitate their work by helping them organize their questions and data, providing them with resources, teaching research skills, and integrating the teaching of basic skills into their meaningful work. To summarize the project approach, I have included the objectives for engaging in project investigations regardless of the content area. Notice that within these objectives, you see explicit ways in which children are actively engaged in critical thinking. The general objectives for project investigations include:

1. Students will engage in an in-depth study of a topic.
2. Students will pursue firsthand investigations.
   a. Students will engage actively in data collection.
   b. Students will become more proficient in organizing data.
   c. Students will learn and utilize different modes for representing data.

3. Students will think critically and reflectively.
   a. Students will engage actively in discussions of the topic, exchange ideas, debate, and so forth.
   b. Students will formulate questions.
   c. Students will evaluate their experiences in many ways and participate in culminating activities.

4. Students will relive and renew experiences they have had with various subject domains.
5. Students will increase their ability to use primary and secondary resources.
6. Students will increase their vocabulary.
7. Students will learn and apply new modes of inquiry including questioning and hypothesizing, reforming of hypotheses, interviewing, surveying, and observing.
8. Students will increase their modes of representing their ideas (observational drawings, graphs, Venn diagrams, displays).
9. Students will uncover facts and principles in various subject domains.
10. Students will be exposed to numerous and varied instructional strategies such as the following:
    a. whole-group instruction and discussion;

   b. small-group instruction and discussion;

   c. interviews with experts;

   d. field trips;

   e. field studies;

   f. student-initiated activities such as constructions, surveys, and representations;

   g. personal conversations with teachers or other student experts; and

   h. experimentation.

11. Students will strengthen their dispositions to be interested in relevant and worthwhile phenomena.

The Project Approach is deeply rooted in the larger movement of progressive education and has taken many different forms throughout the 20th century. For a quick reference to more information about the Project Approach, I suggest visiting the Web site developed by Sylvia Chard at http://www.projectapproach.org or the one hosted by the Early Childhood and Parenting Collaborative (ECAP) at the University of Illinois at Urbana-Champaign at http://ecap.crc.uiuc.edu.

One may find aspects of project work in many different types of early childhood programs, including Head Start programs, which are adopting The Creative Curriculum for Preschool model. In this published curriculum (Heroman, 2005), project work is encouraged with mini-lessons called *study starters*. The study starters help teachers to guide investigations. More on the Head Start program will be discussed below.

Study starters are just one aspect of The Creative Curriculum for Preschool model. Another important key feature is the process by which the teachers use computerized assessment checklists to keep track of progress and growth on basic cognitive, physical, and emotional domains. If early childhood programs purchase this system, teachers may keep individual child data in computerized portfolios. More information about the model, the study starters, and other tools the model employs can be found at http://www.teachingstrategies.com/page/preschool.cfm.

Regardless of what curriculum is used, parents should seek information about the ways that teachers keep track of how students progress. Most early childhood programs should have individual student portfolios, work sampling systems, or assessment checklists with work samples to document growth. A well-developed assessment program informs teachers about how to individualize instruction. Due to the uneven nature of a young child's development, it is absolutely essential that assessment is ongoing and continuous. In programs that use the Project Approach or The Creative Curriculum for Preschool model, documentation of children's growth is integral and key to demonstrating and understanding what children are learning and experiencing.

Montessori Schools

Montessori schools are based on principles of child development and Maria Montessori's belief that knowledge is based on children's perceptions of the world. She believed that children's senses had to be trained and thus created materials and activities to train the senses. Most Montessori schools today reflect her philosophies by allowing children to engage in the Montessori materials that are designed for different developmental levels.

Teachers carefully manipulate the environment to create contexts for children to grow by using the appropriate materials. Montessori environments also are influenced by Maria Montessori's belief in the importance of teaching practical, as well as academic, skills. The environment and materials often are arranged by subject matter and students move about the room engaging in different subject matter activities. In some schools today this belief has been translated into students moving along a set curriculum at their own pace.

Following the beliefs of Maria Montessori, Montessori preschools should look and feel like home. You would more likely see paintings of great masters on the walls than the paintings and drawings of young children. This is intentional to make the walls look more like family living rooms, rather than school classrooms. You also would tend to see children separated by age groups instead of combined classes of 3- and 4-year-olds. Naturally, the interpretation of Montessori schools looks different in each setting. Montessori schools should have a certified Montessori teacher and or administrator. Parents are encouraged to visit the school before making any decisions about whether or not their child might thrive there. To read more about the Montessori method, I suggest going to the Montessori Web site: http://www.montessori.edu.

Reggio Emilia Approach

Already in this book, I have referred many times to the influences of the preprimary schools in Reggio Emilia, Italy, to early education in the United States. Most significantly, I have shared how the environments in those schools have influenced my own work and how we have incorporated their ideas into the classrooms of University Primary School at the University of Illinois (see Figures 3 and 4 for examples of how we have incorporated this approach into our school setting).

In 1991, *Newsweek* named the schools of Reggio Emilia as some of the best early childhood schools in the world (Kantrowitz & Wingert). Philosophically, the schools of Reggio Emilia, Italy, designed by Louis Malaguzzi, are similar to those of Maria Montessori's design. The Reggio Emilia approach comes from more than 40 infant-toddler and preschools that are state operated in the city of Reggio Emilia, Italy. Influenced by Montessori's attention to the environment, the preschools of Reggio Emilia take the stance that the environment is the "third teacher."

Parents who visit preschool programs inspired by the schools in Reggio Emilia might see an attention to the visual arts as a graphic language for children to represent their thinking processes and express their creativity. They might find more natural elements in the children's environments and recyclable materials for students to use, such as those shown in Figures 5 and 6. They would see documentation boards with students' experiences described in detail with conversation and photographs. Finally, they would see evidence of students' engagement in long-term projects, with many activities of the children visibly in process.

There are many early childhood programs across the United States that have been influenced by the schools in Reggio Emilia. These programs pay particular attention to the aesthetics of the environment, the role of the teacher as a facilitator of learning, and the important goal of involving parents and families in the work of the children. There are an abundance of books and resources on the Reggio Emilia approach. Most can be accessed through the Web site for Reggio Children: http://zerosei.comune. re.it/inter/reggiochildren.htm.

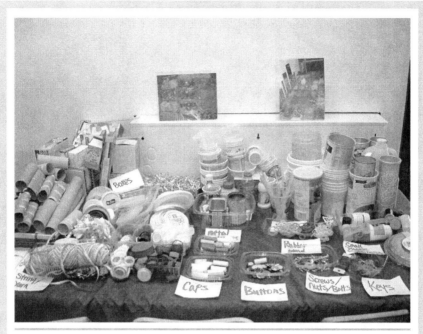

Figure 3. The University Primary School treasures from home table, implementing strategies used in Reggio Emilia schools.

Figure 4. A University Primary School student's self-portrait, created using various materials collected using the Reggio Emilia approach.

Figure 5. A typical display of art materials outside a Reggio Emilia school in Italy.

Figure 6. An art center outside of a Reggio Emilia school in Italy.

Waldorf Schools

Waldorf schools were started in 1919 by Rudolf Steiner, who developed his schools based on the philosophy of meeting the needs of the whole child and incorporating the arts as a way to instill the love of learning. The environment in Waldorf schools is rich with student artwork, and the curriculum includes many hands-on practical experiences. Preschool Waldorf schools have a home-like environment (much like Montessori), but the walls are filled with student work—showing the value that the Waldorf schools place on the arts and creative expression.

According to the Association of Waldorf Schools of North America (AWSNA; n.d.), preschool and kindergarten children primarily learn through imagination and imitation. The school system's goal for kindergarten children includes learning to revere all living things and developing a sense of wonder about the world. Activities in the preschool and kindergarten years include:

- storytelling, puppetry, creative play;
- singing, eurythmy (movement);
- games and finger plays;
- painting, drawing, and beeswax modeling;
- baking and cooking, nature walks; and
- foreign language and circle time for festival and seasonal celebrations. (AWSNA, n.d., ¶ 5)

Three words characterize Waldorf education: head, heart, and hands. Activities in the schools tend to engage children not only in academic learning, but also in affective and aesthetic domains. Although there are no Waldorf schools in my local area, apparently, there is a large Waldorf movement in the United States.

Parents may access the Association of Waldorf Schools in North America for more information (http://www.awsna.org/awsna.html). Another good site, operated by AWSNA, is http://www.whywaldorfworks.org/02_W_Education/faq_about.asp. This site includes a long list of frequently asked questions about the school system, along with a link to a site providing an introduction to Waldorf education.

Early Childhood At-Risk Programs

Across the country, public schools are mandated to provide federally and state-funded free access to preschool for children who have specific risk factors that inhibit their potential achievement. Although each school district may define its own risk factors, they generally include children who come from low-income homes (as defined by poverty levels in the United States), who are raised by a single parent, who are classified as English Language Learners (ELL), and those who have a developmental delay or other disability.

Many local school districts support students from low-income families by providing assistance by federally regulated means, including bus transportation to and from school sites, free or reduced meals, and in some cases, assistance with necessary school supplies or uniforms. Contact your local school district to inquire about its prekindergarten programs and the opportunities available to low-income families in your area. Another good option for low-income families is the Head Start program.

Head Start

Children from low-income households may be the most in need of preschool. According to The Century Foundation

(2000), studies of high-quality childcare programs have proved to be most beneficial to children from economically disadvantaged households. The Head Start program is one of the most well-known preschool programs working with children from low-income households. This program, which began in 1965 and was estimated to serve more than 900,000 children in 2003, targets the poorest children and families. In 2005, the U.S. Department of Health and Human Services noted that 75% of the children in Head Start programs lived in families who fell 100% below the federal poverty line (at $16,090 during that year).

Head Start aims to improve a child's cognitive development while attending to other issues that affect learning, including overall health and wellness. The Children's Defense Fund (2005), which supports the Head Start program, noted that the program also addresses the family's unmet needs, including job training, housing assistance, health care, family counseling, and emotional support, in its work toward achieving three big goals for each family: health services, social services, and parent involvement. Within these goals, Head Start aims to provide each child with medical, dental, and mental healthcare, immunizations, and hot meals; parent education, crisis intervention, and transportation and housing assistance; and programs wherein parents take part in what's going on the classroom, serve on policy councils, and receive necessary job training, literacy and language assistance, and economic stability.

In addition to these services, Head Start works consistently toward achieving cognitive development for the youngsters it serves. The Children's Defense Fund (2005) claimed that Head Start's programs allow its graduates to make "substantial progress in kindergarten," learning vocabulary and letter recognition, math skills, and writing skills relative to the national average for that age group (p. 3).

More information about Head Start can be found by visiting http://www.acf.hhs.gov/programs/hsb or calling the federal government's Early Childhood Learning and Knowledge Center at 1-866-763-6481. Another good resource is the National Head Start Association (http://www.nhsa.org), which can be contacted at 703-739-0875. If you come from a low-income household, I strongly suggest you contact both your local school district and the Head Start program to find out what options are available in your local area.

English Language Learners

In their compendium on English Language Learners, *What Works: Promising Practices for Improving the School Readiness of English Language Learners*, the organization Ready at Five (2004), noted that the U.S. Census Bureau estimates that by the year 2030, diverse ethnic and racial groups will comprise 40% of the U.S. population. Naturally, as a result of this growth, more and more children under age 5 will be considered English Language Learners (students who are not proficient in speaking English; ELL). The numbers of English Language Learners already are growing significantly:

> Between 1992 and 2002, the ELL student population increased 72 percent. In 2002, there were 3,977,819 public school students (grades K–12) throughout the nation who were learning the English language. This represents nearly 8.4 percent of all students in grades K–12, of which nearly 70 percent are elementary school students. (Ready at Five, 2004, p. 13)

Ready at Five (2004) noted that although the majority of English Language Learners primarily speak Spanish, more than 460 languages are spoken by ELL students nationwide. Organizations like Ready at Five stress the need for ELL students to receive proper early childhood educations because of the discrepancies between such students and their English-speaking peers that appear later in life: 76% of third-grade ELL students were reading below grade level in 2004, and in that same year, 52.9% of eighth-grade ELL students were reading below grade level (Ready at Five, 2004).

The Ready at Five (2004) organization also noted that an overwhelming 77% of ELL students come from low-income backgrounds, making the need for their education even greater. Many such students are served by the Head Start program, which recognizes the increase itself and frequently disseminates information about best practices for working with these students to its teachers.

What can parents of students who are English Language Learners do? The U.S. Department of Health and Human Services (2005b) suggested enrolling in family literacy classes and participating in parent-child activities is one good option. Ready at Five (2004) encouraged schools to respect parents' cultures and establish rapport between parents and schools. Parents of ELL students can become involved in many of the same ways that parents of English-speaking students can by volunteering time and donations. Most importantly parents of ELL students should maintain as much communication as possible with their child's teacher (potentially through a school interpreter at first).

Parents of English-speaking children should note that ELL students may be present in their child's classrooms, especially in public schools or Head Start programs. In some states, such as

Texas, bilingual programs in public schools are growing rapidly. In an article on the increase of bilingual prekindergarten and kindergarten programs in Dallas, Ayres (2005) reported that 55,000 students in Texas are being served in bilingual prekindergarten classrooms. In many Texas school districts, such as Dallas ISD, some ELL students are on waiting lists to be served in these classrooms (Ayres, 2005). Even though Dallas ISD has retained those bilingual classrooms, many are moving to a new type of classroom: the dual immersion classroom.

Some kindergartens and prekindergartens like Dallas ISD serve a dual immersion capacity, wherein ELL and English-speaking students together learn in both Spanish and English. Unger (2001) reported that such programs, which began in the 1960s, took off in the 1970s, when many English-speaking parents recognized the benefit of their children learning a second language in a dual immersion classroom. In 2001, Unger had found 200 dual immersion programs across the United States. The Dallas dual-immersion classrooms include half a day of instruction in Spanish and half a day in English, from kindergarten to the sixth grade, with the subjects taught in each language varying regularly so that children do not get comfortable learning only the subjects covered in their native language (Ayres, 2007). Tabors and López (2005) noted that "bilingualism can be beneficial for children's language and literacy development, for family communication and functioning, and for children's feelings of self-worth," further emphasizing that bilingual citizens often receive opportunities not available to those who can only speak one language.

Thus, if you are an English-speaking parent concerned about future study of foreign languages, you might consider finding and enrolling your child in a dual immersion preschool or kindergarten program. Otherwise, if you are an English-speaking parent whose child has classmates who are ELL students or students whose parents do not speak English, do your part to respect the cultures of those students and teach your children to respect the other child's cultures. Do not let language serve as a barrier between your child and his or her classmates (and potential friends). Encourage respect for one another's differences and show that respect by maintaining friendly relations and communication (when possible) with the other parents. Most importantly, recognize that you all have some things in common: letting go of your children into a teacher's hands each day, seeing your child's discovery and enthusiasm of new learning experiences, and helping your child learn the strategies that will ultimately help him or her to lead a happy and fulfilled life.

Children With Disabilities

Most public school districts have to prioritize who will receive their early childhood services and some of these programs have become almost exclusively for children with disabilities who are governed by the Individuals with Disabilities Education Improvement Act (IDEA; 2004). Some such classrooms have become segregated programs where the deficits of the children often are attended to over the children's strengths and interests. These programs have strong parent components because parents of children with disabilities by law have input into their child's placement and programming.

IDEA 2004 provides for infants, toddlers, and preschoolers with disabilities to receive programming services under two potential service plans—the Individualized Education Program (IEP) or the Individualized Family Service Plan (IFSP). Weinfeld and Davis (2008) noted that because children from birth to age

5 are entitled to what is called a free appropriate public education (or FAPE) under federal law, the public school system must
provide these children with special services in the school setting.
Children who have minor developmental issues, if those developmental delays affect the child's ability to do the same thing
his or her peers can do at a developmentally appropriate level,
also are eligible for special services in the public school setting
(Weinfeld & Davis, 2008).

Each program may have a different philosophy or follow a
different curriculum, but I have found many public school programs to be heavily populated with students with special needs.
And, while the education in these programs provides necessary
services to children with special needs, as parents, you would
want to make sure that your child's strengths also are addressed
in such placements. I have participated in many IEP meetings
where the focus of the child's "program" was speech, physical,
or occupational therapy, and not on emergent literacy activities
or social play. No matter where a child is placed, or what type of
program is developed for a child, the needs of the whole child
—physical, social, emotional, and cognitive—must be addressed
through a strengths-based approach.

Advantages or Disadvantages of Programs and Curricular Models

Parents might ask if there are advantages or disadvantages
to different approaches to curriculum or to the different types of
preschool settings. I believe that question lies in the eyes of the
beholder. Cultural and family values play a huge role in determin-
ing what is "best" for their child. Therefore, where one family
might want a more teacher-directed, individually paced program

for their child, another family might want learning to take place in more informal social peer-group situations. For example, my neighbor's children were in a local Montessori program where they worked on letters and sound worksheets when they were in preschool. That is not what I wished for my children, but my neighbors delighted in their own children's success with that approach. Some parents visit University Primary School and love the fact that children can make their own choices (that are carefully controlled and manipulated by the teacher, of course) for the first hour of each morning. Other parents see the choice time and feel as though it may be too chaotic for their children. I believe that is why it is so difficult to recommend a specific program or a curricular approach for one child and why instead, it is important for parents to look at the whole picture—not only the setting, but the interrelationship between the philosophy and the curricular approach of the program and their own values, views on learning, and knowledge of their own child.

Conclusion

I recently toured a brand-new corporate-owned early childhood center. I coveted the spacious entry with high ceilings and windows. How I wish I had that at University Primary School! But, I was disappointed to see that outside one of the toddler classrooms were 10 snowmen looking exactly alike (this was January in Illinois); hanging from the ceilings in all of the classrooms were placards saying Art, Reading, Construction, and Dramatic Play (if you want young children to read, you need to put the text at eye level); and some original paintings were arranged seemingly randomly on bulletin boards. More frequently, bulletin boards were covered with the alphabet or store-purchased letters and numbers.

And, while the environment bothered me, what most caught my attention on my way out the front door (at 3 p.m.) were two young 5-year-old girls who had come to the center for afterschool care sitting on the entryway couch and chair. I stopped to ask them what they were doing there and they told me they were waiting for their teacher who was on break. I wondered if they had any books to read or could they play any games? No, they told me they had to leave their stuff in their classroom. One of the corporation's Executive Directors was sitting behind the large entryway desk working on her computer and overhead my conversation. (Why she was not getting these girls something to do, or why she couldn't have stayed in the classroom for the teacher who went on break, I do not know.)

I left the center wondering if this wait time takes place every day. The two girls acted like it was a routine occurrence. It is difficult to say exactly what parents might want to see in a classroom because they may have different goals for their children, but what we certainly do not want to see is children waiting on adults. Children should be actively engaged with each other or with teachers in learning about the world around them.

Chapter 5

Strengthening Partnerships Between School and Home

AMY runs into the preschool classroom—she can't wait to get to school to see her friends and her teachers. She opens the door, and then begins dropping her coat, her hat, and her gloves on the floor as she runs to the choice board to see what she will do first in the morning. Her mother, holding her 18-month-old brother tries to keep up, bends over to pick up Amy's hat, coat, and gloves, almost dropping the toddler, and takes the clothing apparel to the coat hook with Amy's name clearly marked. After the mother has put Amy's things carefully in her cubby, she gives her a kiss goodbye and leaves her happily engaged.

This is a typical morning drop-off scene in the preschool classroom. Although the child is wonderfully happy, the mother has not supported her in the responsibility of taking off her own coat and hanging it up on her own at her cubby. Although a seemingly simple task, imagine the preschool classroom if every child dropped his or her belongings at the door! Strengthening partnerships between home and school include working toward common goals, maintaining ongoing open communication, and supporting the teachers and the school in their efforts to nurture and teach your child. In this chapter, specific ways for you to support your child in his or her new environment and develop positive relationships with your child's teachers will be discussed.

Shared Goals

As mentioned earlier, although many preschool settings may be implementing developmentally appropriate practices, it is important to select the school where you feel your goals match that of the philosophy of the school. Having shared goals for your child is the first step into developing positive relationships with the teachers and other staff at the school. When you have meetings with your child's teachers, remember that they want to see your child grow and develop in appropriate ways just as you do. Rest assured that the teachers you put your trust in have an interest in helping your child grow to his or her potential. Teachers and parents want what is best for the children in that preschool classroom—keep that thought as the common denominator of all other communications you may have. Now of course, "what's best" may be negotiable—be prepared to learn from your child's teachers. Also be prepared to understand differences between the home and school environment.

Suppose you do not care at home if your child hangs his or her coat up on a hook. Well, you may be a bit surprised when the teacher requests that when you come to school, you allow your child to hang his or her own coat up on the hook. You're happy to do that for your child because you are getting ready to leave him for 3 hours. On the other hand, the teacher is trying to help your child become independent for the times when he or she goes out to play and comes back inside when you are not there.

Katz (1995) suggests that as much as it seems that teachers of young children "mother" their students, the roles of teachers and parents are significantly different. She said,

> Parents have a right to protect their own child's cultural/ethnic uniqueness and to ask of the teacher that special consideration, as appropriate for their child. The teacher is responsible not only for every individual in the group, but for the life of the group as a unit. (p. 176)

Our preschool classrooms are becoming more linguistically and ethnically diverse than they have ever been in the past. It is natural that families may have different goals and expectations for their children than teachers whose backgrounds are vastly different from their own. The key to any type of partnership between parents and teachers is respect. In high-quality early childhood programs, parents should feel comfortable answering the following questions:

In my relationships with the staff, are they:
- Primarily respectful, rather than patronizing or controlling?
- Accepting, open, inclusive, and tolerant, rather than rejecting, blaming, and prejudiced?
- Respectful of my goals and values for my child?
- Welcoming contacts that are ongoing and frequent rather than rare and distant? (Katz, 1995, p. 124)

Being respectful does not always mean that teachers and parents have to agree on everything. For example, we do know that different cultures place different values on aspects of childhood. Independence with self-help skills for example, is a typical American goal for young children. How parents teach their children to respect the authority of adults also differs across cultures. Understanding differences and establishing the expectations for the child in the preschool setting are important ways for parents and teachers to build partnerships that will benefit the children.

Communication

Maria always came to school in a beautiful dress. She loved to twirl around and see her dress float high around her waist. It was while she was doing this that the other children quickly discovered Maria did not wear underwear. Her teacher came to me to ask for advice about how to mention this to Maria's parent.

Communication is not always easy—both teachers and parents must be thoughtful and strategic about how to approach each other with tough subjects. In this case, Maria's mother acknowledged that she did not send her to school in underwear because at home she always takes it off. The teacher explained how it might not be sanitary for Maria to be sitting on the carpet at group time without any underwear. Then, the teacher promptly went out and bought several extra pair of underwear just in case Maria came back without her own. In most cases, Maria's mother remembered the underwear, but the teacher was prepared either way. Sometimes there are subjects that are difficult for parents to communicate to teachers and vice versa. The key to ongoing communication is honesty.

When parents try to keep things from the teachers or staff members, it never works. Children are the first to tell you that their parents fought the night before, the dog died, the fish was buried in the toilet, or their sister ate poison and had to be rushed to the hospital. These major events in a child's life come out naturally in conversation while they play with their peers, or after they have a tantrum and are talking with the teacher. It was no surprise to me that my son's journal entry about the night his mom nearly burned down the kitchen resulted in a telephone call to me from his teacher. It was a traumatic night— for all of us.

Sometimes when children show so many signs of stress the teachers wonder, "What is going on at home that results in such anxiety?" The teachers are not trying to blame the parents; on the contrary, they want to know how to help the child. So, from a teacher's perspective, always inform the teacher of anything that might cause the child to be tired, anxious, or basically "out of sorts," for school.

By letting the teacher know about the circumstances surrounding the stress, the teacher can help the child identify his or her emotions and find outlets for expressing them. I often ask parents why they did not tell us about an incident or specific circumstances that were making the child less stable at home. Parents will say that they do not think their children will have a problem concerning the incident once they get to school. Some children, just like adults, carry their stress with them. Although an incident started at home, the child may not be able to stop thinking about it at school. The same is true if a child has a fight or has an unpleasant experience at school. The child might then lash out at the parents once he is home. In both cases, teachers and parents must learn to communicate whether or not there have been any problems or memorable experiences (either positive or negative) that just may impact the child's life at school or home.

Do not feel defensive or threatened if your child's teacher asks if there are any circumstances at home that may be contributing to your child's behavior. Teachers generally recognize signs of child stress and just want to know if the parent sees some of the same signs at home as they see at school, including:

- increase in aggressive or withdrawn behavior;
- increase in distractibility;
- loss of appetite;
- clingy (crying when parent leaves);
- increased sleepiness, falling asleep during instructional time;
- increase in tantrums or loss of self-control (crying); and
- increase in self-stimulating behaviors, including chewing on piece of clothing, twirling when sitting down in group time, or drumming or twisting one's hands.

An honest discussion with the teacher about anything going on at home might help the teacher understand the child's behavior and help the child understand that there are some strategies to use when feeling sad, stressed, lonely, tired, or anxious. In some cases, the teacher may have information about additional resources to share with parents and families. No information is too small or insignificant to pass on to the child's teacher when you drop your child off for the day. If the child woke up early, or could not sleep because he's afraid of thunderstorms, let the teachers know the next morning. Sharing information helps to bridge the two environments.

If the teacher knows the child is sleepy, she might not worry about the child not wanting to play and give more time for the child to just sit and relax. Teachers only can respond to the needs of the child if they are informed about those needs. So, communication has to be ongoing and two-way. Parents share with the teachers, and teachers should share information frequently with the parents.

In addition to drop-off and pick-up times where they can communicate in person, parents should expect to see a weekly newsletter or some form of communication home that tells about the activities that the children are doing. Some early childhood programs now have active Web sites where parents can see daily photographs, videos, or text of the children's activities. In some daycare centers, there is a camera and parents with passwords can log onto a Web site to watch their child in "real time."

The communication patterns that are established should make parents feel comfortable and informed. Parents can support their children by reading the information that is sent home in those backpacks. Instead of asking your child, "How did your day go?" or "What did you do today?" use the newsletters, Web site, or videos to ask specific questions. For example, you might ask, "What can you tell me about the story your teacher read today?" or "I noticed there was paint available today, how did you use the paint?" or "What friends did you play with outside." These specific questions engage the child in conversation and give you an opportunity to communicate not only with your child's teachers, but also with him about his day.

One final note about communication—if there is something important that you want your child's teachers to know about your child, do not be afraid to tell them. This of course includes information about food allergies, things that make your child anxious (like going to the bathroom in front of a stranger), or activities your child loves to do. My son's first preschool teacher when he was 2 years old listened to our concerns about his small size, heard us worry aloud about whether or not he could play as rough and tough as some of the other boys, knew that I wanted to be informed whether or not he ate snack and how much he slept, and also listened to us as we told her that he was interested in guitars and had memorized some Peter, Paul, and Mary songs. She built a small platform, put Christmas lights around the platform, and brought out pretend guitars for my son to lead a band. To this day, I wonder how this very early experience of leading a band on stage impacted his future career as a musician.

A family-friendly environment reaches out to parents in many different ways. Parents should be greeted and feel comfortable entering their child's classroom. The teacher should be implementing best practices all of the time, not just when there are parent volunteers in the room. Parents should expect to hear "good stories" about their children, and not only called or brought into the school to discuss problem behaviors.

Parent Involvement

An outdated notion of parent involvement meant that parents had to come into the classroom and participate in classroom activities or attend parent conferences. Parent involvement is much broader than that. Parent involvement includes all of the things parents do to support their child in a school setting. It can be anything from helping your child get enough sleep each night before school to being the field trip driver with extra booster

Table 9

Sample Parent Volunteer Activities

In the Classroom	Outside the Classroom
Read with children and discuss books.	Bind monthly journals.
Cook with a small group of children.	Organize a book order.
Help with an art activity.	Type teachers' documentation (students' brainstorming ideas).
Teach a foreign language.	Put children's work in art frames.
Hang children's work up in displays.	Shop for items the teacher requests.
Take dictation of children's stories.	Go to the public library and collect books on a topic for the teacher.
Play a game with children.	Sew clothes for dramatic play.
Act as the content expert and be interviewed by the children on a topic that is being investigated.	Help plan field studies and bring in resources that match the topic children are investigating.

seats in the car. Wise early childhood teachers have systems for including parents in their planning, their activities, and their evaluation of their program. They have tasks that parents can do at home and at school. Table 9 lists some sample activities that parent volunteers often do at University Primary School.

Parent Support

Parent involvement also means supporting the teachers and the goals of the school at home. For example, make sure you give your child a consistent, warm, and loving bedtime routine that will lead to your child getting enough sleep to do well in school the next day.

When my children were young, they both looked forward to the bedtime routine. It started with a bath (which as I said before, was Dad's job if he was home). Then we read books together out loud. Sometimes my sons read to me, other times, I read to them, depending on the choice of book, and the stages of their reading. When my husband was out of town, I managed two stories at once by giving my older child a book on tape. He loved picking out the story he was going to listen to. Sometimes, he followed the oral version by reading the book along with the narrator. Other times, he listened in the dark and fell asleep. After reading to the children, when all was calm, quiet, and safe, I asked about their day or had them tell me one nice thought before going to sleep. Going to bed was never a struggle for my children because it became their favorite time of day—they had their parents' attention and they were enjoying time together.

The ritual of the bedtime routine served many purposes— sharing the joy of reading, spending time with the family, and getting to know about their day. Today I worry whether or not many of our young children are getting that same type of bedtime routine. At University Primary School, some students tell their teachers about television shows that they are watching with their parents—not all of them appropriate to watch, but some that also are very late for 3–5-year-olds. The teachers always say, "No wonder!" when the child is fussy and irritable in school.

Some of our students get the same amount of sleep as their parents, and not more. Their parents simply allow them to fall asleep on the couch (in front of TV) when they are ready. If you want your children to be alert and fresh for the new day, make sure you support those habits by providing the environment that teaches the importance of nightly routines that lead to healthy minds and bodies.

Support the goals of the school at home by using some of the same language for expectations. Give your child choice language and encourage him to problem solve just like he is encouraged to use and do at school. Remember that punishment does not teach appropriate behavior. Support the teachers by using similar phrases and techniques to demonstrate that natural and logical consequences happen at home too, and not just at school.

Become interested in the topic that students are learning about. Read books and engage your child in conversation about the topic. Take your child to the library and look up information about a topic together and then discuss how you might share that information with other students in your child's class who also might be interested. One way to become invested in the topics your child and his or her classmates are learning about is to ask your child's teacher if you and other parent volunteers can help implement a project. Also, ask your child to tell you about the projects or investigations and look for ways you can help. Often, preschools encourage parents to share various aspects of their native cultures, ethnicities, or religions in order to increase an appreciation for diversity among their students. Parents can take an integral role in such investigations and projects, both by helping their child learn about their particular cultural background and by providing means by which their child's peers can learn about the culture.

One project we have implemented at University Primary School is called Food of Our Families. This project was popular not only with the children in our school, but also with their parents. During the autumn of the year the project was conducted, the children did an investigative study of harvests and fruits and vegetables. Their interest in food remained the next semester, and teaching a culturally and linguistically diverse population, the teachers in our school were curious about the children's family customs and traditions. We decided to incorporate the students' current interest in foods with our desire to learn more about their backgrounds, leading to the Food of Our Families project.

First, we had students draw pictures and tell their classmates about the types of food their families ate. Then, we asked for parent involvement on several trips to grocery stores and local restaurants. We brought this learning back to the school by setting up a grocery store, complete with multicultural food items (many of which were donated by parents; see Figure 7). Parent volunteers also came into the classroom every other day to cook and talk about their family's favorite foods. We also hosted a potluck luncheon, asking parents to bring in foods that represented their family's cultural heritage.

Many schools do similar projects with their students, but if your child's school does not do so, you might consider suggesting something to your child's teacher. You could preface such a suggestion by mentioning your child's interest in his or her culture, such as, "Maya has begun taking dance lessons to learn some of the traditional dances of our family's Latino heritage. She would love to be able to share what she's learned with her classmates—Do you have any ideas for projects or times when she might be able to do so?" or "Jin recently has discovered that

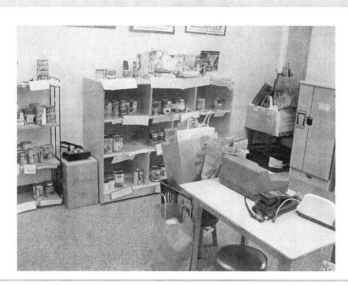

Figure 7. The multicultural grocery store students set up with donations of food from their families for the University Primary School Food of Our Families Project.

he loves to eat sushi and has become quite adept at helping his mother and I make it at home. If you're ever interested in having us come in and make a demonstration of how we make sushi for the children, we would be happy to do so."

You don't have to wait for specific projects to come around either to get involved with your child's school; you can support your child's involvement in the school by embracing the curriculum and philosophy of the school. If your child's school has hands-on types of activities, what types of activities can you do at home that reflect or reciprocate those activities? For example, if your child loved making the salt-based play dough at school and talks about it constantly, how can you help him make it at home? Suppose your child talks about a specific activity he did the day before. When you come into the school the next morning, take some time to look at what he did and have him share how he did it. Praise effort instead of quality of product. Often times, young children will have great ideas, but lack the skills to implement them. Show them your are more than pleased with their ideas and problem-solving abilities, and do not be disappointed if you do not recognize the child's masterpiece the way you envisioned it should be.

Conclusion

Strengthening partnerships between school and home involve both parents and teachers working together on behalf of the child. Relationships matter. Recognize the importance of the relationship between parents and teachers, and do not hold questions or concerns to yourself and let them fester until you are so mad that you cannot be civil or professional with the program staff. Act immediately to resolve any conflicts and use structured problem-solving skills to do it. Your child will benefit from frequent, friendly, and positive interactions between you and his teachers.

Chapter 6

Letting Go

Making the Transition From Home to School

The greatest gifts you can give your children are the roots of responsibility and the wings of independence. —Dennis Waitley

I can still remember my oldest son's first day of kindergarten. I walked him to school with my video camera in tow. When we got to the playground, there were hundreds of students standing outside waiting for the first bell of the year to sound. There were a few other parents walking with their children to school. When my son saw all of the students lined up by the door, he ran ahead of me, never even looking back! By the time I turned on the camera, all I could see was his backside running into the massive lines of other children. I realized then that going to school was only a traumatic experience for me, not him.

Five minutes after all of the children had entered the school, there I was looking around wondering where were all of the other parents? Why was I still lingering? What had just happened? Who did I have to commiserate with about my "losing" those early years of "mommy time?" Or, was I upset that my son was about to be acculturated into that institution called *school*? That first day of kindergarten was a milestone—for me. I went straight to a coffee shop and reflected upon just how lucky I was my son felt so confident to go to school, and also how quickly the time had passed between his traumatic early birth and his first day of school. And, it did not get any easier when my second child left for kindergarten, because then I knew he was my youngest and I would never experience those early years again.

That feeling of needing someone to talk to about the quick passage of time and whether or not a child will have a good beginning to many years of school has never left me. At University Primary School, on the first day of school, I always open a conference room with coffee and snacks for parents so they can share their worries and reflections together. Last fall, I only had one mother in tears. I consoled her every 10 minutes or so with the update on her son, who was doing "just fine" in the preschool classroom. Although he cried initially as his mother departed, within minutes, he was engaged with one of the preschool teachers reading a book, while his mother was sobbing over coffee.

Beginning preschool or kindergarten can be a very emotional time for parents. Not only do they worry about their child, but they also may be transitioning into new lifestyles and changes in routines. Change has impact. Suddenly, you do not know everything that may be influencing your child. In the early years of preschool and kindergarten, children may not be able to express all that happens to them in one day. And so, letting go of this control over your child's experiences may be difficult.

Preschoolers also experience changes in their lives. Many preschoolers have siblings during this time period, or begin to go between early childhood centers (preschool in the morning, daycare in the afternoon). The childbearing years also may create pressure on families to raise their incomes, change their jobs, or move to larger housing as the family grows. Parents may ease these transitions for themselves and their children by talking about them, getting prepared for the changes, and most importantly, being positive about the new things to come. This chapter will focus on specific strategies that facilitate your child's transition from home to school, and hopefully give the perspective that these changes are positive.

Facilitating Transitions to School

Because the unknown can be scary to a child, the first suggestion for facilitating a transition between home and school, or a familiar daycare and school, is to make the school a familiar environment. Visit the preschool before sending your child. On your visit to the school, introduce your child to his future teacher and to other staff that might be there. Show your child the bathrooms (try them out, too), the classroom, and the playground. It would be great if you could spend some time on the playground with your child, familiarizing him or her with the apparatus, the boundaries, and the endless possibilities for fun.

Many early childhood centers have orientation programs for both the adults and children. Sometimes the children begin school in small groups and only a few of the children attend on the first day, followed by another small group on the second day. Be sure that you and your child participate in those types of orientation programs. In an adult orientation, the school staff may remind parents of their policies, including expectations for drop-off and pick-up routines, curricular models used, discipline policies, celebration of holidays, staff development, and rules such as a 24-hour wellness policy. Be sure to ask questions you may have. New health requirements in some states do not allow parents to bring any food or snacks that are not store-bought to class. So, do not be surprised if you can no longer bring cookies or cupcakes from home to celebrate birthdays. Hopefully, your child's preschool will have some form of family handbook or written book of policies and procedures that you can read before selecting the school. Being familiar with the expectations of the school will help you make the necessary provisions for your child.

There often is a distinction made between orientation programs (which happen only in the beginning) and transition, which happens gradually. Although you may take your child several times to the school to help him become familiar with the environment, you will want to continually provide support for your child by telling him that you are confident he will do well there. Your demeanor and attitude toward the new environment is critical to your child feeling secure, comfortable, and happy there.

A Positive Attitude—
Building Self-Confidence

Many parents ask me how I know if their children will be happy at University Primary School. I know from experience that if their parents are happy, then their children usually are happy. If parents are skeptical or unsure about whether or not the preschool is a good place for their child, the child will sense it. Therefore, one of the best ways to get your child off to a good start is to talk positively about the school, the teachers, the environment, and all of the experiences your child will have there. When you feel confident about your children being happy and successful, it helps to build their confidence. You do not need to be unrealistic and tell your children that they will never have any problems at school. You need to tell them that if there are problems, there are plenty of people there to help them solve them.

Acknowledge your child's feelings of being unsure, worried, or scared, and then talk about the teachers, the director, and the assistants who will be there to help him with those worries. There also are children who will feel just as he does, and perhaps he could help them or vice versa. Sometimes it helps children if they bring a token from home with them to school. One favorite example of such a token is a photograph of their family or even their pet that they can put into their pocket. When they are feeling lonely or sad, they can pull it out of their pocket or cubby and smile, knowing that they are not alone.

Practice doing some of the activities that your child will be asked to do at preschool such as washing his or her hands, sitting quietly, hanging up his coat, zipping up his zipper, and so on. Many of the self-help skills that we talked about in the previous chapters need to be practiced before school so that the child can feel confident about doing them independently. Even putting shoes on and off can be difficult to a child if he has never had to do it on his own.

Self-help skills are the very skills that take preschoolers so long to do by themselves that you often want to "do it" for them. They include things such as going to the bathroom, brushing their teeth, getting dressed or undressed, blowing their nose, and wiping their face. At home it might not be a problem when parents try to help. But at school, children need to learn to do these tasks by themselves.

It is not unusual to see preschoolers walking out of the bathroom with their pants still down by their shoes or to see shoes or boots put on the wrong feet. Some parents apologize for the outfit that their children are wearing because they let them pick it out themselves. Remember that when you allow your children to do these tasks on their own, they are building confidence. So, slow down, and don't be in a hurry during the morning dressing routine or the dinner cleanup time. Give your children time to get dressed, wash their hands, or whatever the task may be so they feel that sense of independence when they do something on their own. (And, it may be fine to let them go to school with clothes that don't match or with their shoes on the wrong feet—at least once!)

If your child will be taking a lunch or snack to his preschool, be sure to practice opening thermos bottles, juice cartons, fruit or pudding cups, and vacuum-packed cheese sticks. You would be surprised how difficult food packaging is for children, even when it is meant to go in lunch boxes. If your child is eating lunch outside the home, resist the temptation to inquire about it every day. We have had young children cry at lunch time when we asked them to put their leftover sandwich back in their lunchbox because they did not want to tell their parents that they did not eat it. Sometimes we beg our students to tell their parents what they like and don't like so that their parents do not pack what they will not eat day after day. If at all possible, have your child help make decisions about what is packed or not packed into a snack pack or lunch box. And then, if the whole lunch is not eaten, rest assured, he will not starve. It is possible that the early childhood program served a snack or someone had a birthday treat.

Difficult Separations

If your child is one who holds on to your coat, screams like he is tortured, or runs after you down the hall when you start to leave, do not be or feel embarrassed. Separation anxieties are quite normal and happen to various degrees with most children. Do not let your child's reactions cause you to overreact: Stay calm, reassure your child he or she will be OK, tell your child when you will see him or her next (at lunch, dinner), and then be prepared to allow your child's preschool teacher work the magic of turning your crying child into a classroom helper, within a matter of minutes.

A common pattern of behavior that happens with clingy children is that their parents will linger in the preschool classroom at drop-off time. Therefore, the child is never quite sure when that fearful moment of leaving will happen. For parents who have children who are likely to be anxious about them leaving, I suggest designing a "Departure Routine." For example, in our program, all students must wash their hands upon entering the classroom after hanging up their own coats. Some of our busy parents tell their children they will leave right after their children wash their hands. Other parents may have time to read a book first with their child. Tell your child that you have to go to work or back home right after you read the book together. Whatever you do, do not sneak out. Give your child the satisfaction of waving goodbye and tell him when you will see him next.

A skillful teacher will do her best to ease transitions. She most often takes the child from the parent and shifts his interest into something else. For example, it is not uncommon for one of our teachers to get the "hand-off" from a parent (the signal that the parent wants the teacher to take over), and then have the teacher carry the child into the kitchen to help pre-pare snack or into the storage room to look for something the teacher needs—all the while talking to the child about helping her. Pretty soon, the child is talking and helping and forgetting that she is upset about her parent leaving. If the helper trick won't work, we sometimes read the child's favorite book when the parent leaves, inviting other friends to come and listen. (Of course, the child has to stop crying so that his friends can hear the story too.)

We have found that the sooner the parent says goodbye to the child, the more quickly the child engages with other children. So, even if it seems from the parent's perspective that it would be a "good thing" to stay a while in your child's classroom, remember that it may be preventing your child from peer interactions, which is the reason you may be sending your child to preschool in the first place.

Parents who volunteer in the classroom should be sure to talk to their children about the role they will play when they are in that classroom. In other words, tell them they may be working with other children, helping the teacher, preparing materials outside of the room, in a teacher workroom for example, or supervising groups of children that may not include their own. We have found that children vary in their ability to have their parents in the same room and not be working with them. For some children, it makes no difference at all if their parents are there or not. For others, they change their normal play patterns and cling to their parent. As parents, you may have to change your level of involvement based on how your child manages having you in the classroom.

Reading children's stories that have characters that leave home and go to school is another technique to introduce the feelings and emotions tied to the transition process. My boys both loved the Berenstain Bears series by Stan and Jan Berenstain. Many books in the series describe first-time experiences for the young bears. Parents may want to read *The Berenstain Bears Go to School* to discuss how the young bears feel about leaving home and going to school with other bears. A list of additional children's books dealing with making the transition from home to school can be found in this book's resources section on page 188.

Transitions for Children With Special Needs

Families who have children with special needs may or may not need more support with the transition from home to a preschool environment than other children. However, if families have Individualized Family Service Plans (IFSP), then there are legal provisions (set up under the Individuals with Disabilities Education Act) for making the smooth transition from an IFSP to an Individualized Education Program (IEP). The IFSP is created for families of children birth to age 3 who have identified disabilities and need early intervention services. The IEP is a legal document that articulates services in an educational setting for children 3 to 21 years old.

The IFSP team generally includes the parents, service coordinator, and other related service providers as necessary. These service providers may be occupational or developmental therapists, social workers, or speech pathologists, for example. The IEP team generally consists of parents, the student, regular education teachers, a special education teacher, a school district representative, and other related service providers.

Public schools are required to serve children with disabilities from ages 3–21. At the transition team planning meeting it is important for the parents to share with professionals what they feel their child needs to ease the transition. It also is important to inform the incoming school about health concerns, including allergies, mobility issues (how child should be moved, held, or transitioned in and out of a walker or wheelchair for example), and any other things that the current teachers may be doing to help the child function successfully in a school setting. If a child is in a wheelchair, it is important for the receiving school to examine the accessibility of the classrooms, hallways, bathrooms, playground, and any other place where the child would go to be with his peers. There are some simple ways to make classrooms more accessible, including getting rid of rugs that are difficult to wheel the chair on, putting materials at table height and not too low or too high, making sure there is adequate room to roll the wheelchair between tables and desks, and once in the classroom, making all of the children feel comfortable moving in and around the wheelchair.

Not all children with special needs have disabilities. Over the last few years it seems that more and more children who attend University Primary School have food allergies. Imagine how scary it would be if you sent your child off to school knowing that eating peanuts could kill him. Aware of parents' concerns, we have had to declare our school a "peanut-free zone," and we also have changed our snacks so that all of our children can eat them. That means we no longer can serve snacks with flour, eggs, wheat, nuts, soy, milk, and more. Fortunately, the parents whose child has these allergies shared a list of the foods the child can eat, and we have accommodated the child by serving only what he can eat. We shared our new policy with all of our families, and created new snack menus and cooking activities in the classroom. Last year this child brought his own snack to school, but this year he can eat everything we serve. His parents are appreciative of the steps our program took to be inclusive and accommodating.

If your child has a food allergy, it's imperative that you be upfront and clear about this allergy to your child's school staff. Provide lists of everything your child is allergic to and make multiple copies of this list for the staff to distribute. Make sure the school knows the reaction your child has to the foods and what should be done if something happens and your child accidentally is exposed to the foods. This may require requesting that the school's nurse's office be stocked with the necessary medications or emergency precautions your child will need to receive if exposed.

At the same time, just as your child's teachers should be accommodating to your child's needs, make sure you are polite in informing them about your child's concerns. Provide as much information as possible, and offer to help ease the burden of finding substitute foods by volunteering to bring food your child can eat to school parties or creating a list of all of the school-appropriate foods he or she can eat so that the school can easily change its menus.

When Families Have Special Needs

Children are not the only ones who have special needs when they begin attending preschool. Sometimes families have special needs and may need additional conferences with the administration and staff before school begins. If a parent has a disability and needs help with the drop-off or pick-up routines, he should let the school know. If a parent is going through custody disputes and information needs to be sent to one or both parents, they need to let the staff know. We see many young parents who are stressed and tired. If transitions are not going well, they just need to ask for help. Early childhood educators, if they do not have help on sight, should be able to direct parents to resources. Many communities have local agencies that will provide parents with resources and assistance.

Conclusion

In their book entitled *Social & Emotional Development*, Riley and colleagues (2008) summarized many of the strategies that I have discussed above and give reasons why the strategy helps the child. Rituals and routines provide predictability and build trust. Children feel more control over their environment when they know what happens next. Giving the child a photograph or a stuffed animal (transitional object) allows the child to feel secure as he moves from his home world to the school environment. Encourage your child to engage with another child upon coming into the classroom. This distracts him from the anxiety of separating from you. Sometimes you will need the teacher to distract him with a favorite game or activity. Most of these strategies preschool teachers do naturally and intuitively. But, for a child with problems making transitions, I suggest making an explicit plan that both you and the teacher will follow every day.

Chapter 7

Final Thoughts

Advice is like the snow. The softer it falls, the deeper it sinks into the mind.—Samuel Taylor Coleridge (Blaydes, 2003, p. 91)

THROUGHOUT the book, I have focused on explicit and positive strategies you can use to help your child grow in ways that will help him be happy and successful, not only in preschool, but as he develops throughout his childhood. Most of my lists have been stated as things to try or do. In researching this book I have found many other wonderful resources and lists for parents to use as references. One such pamphlet entitled, *School Readiness: Starting Your Child Off Right* (visit http://www.NCsmartstart.org for more information) from the North Carolina Partnership for Children lists activities for parents to do across the readiness domains: health and physical development, social and emotional development, approaches to learning, communication, and thinking and general knowledge.

The list, almost identical to the items listed on the United Way Calendar I mentioned in the first chapter, includes many ideas similar to those I discussed in the RECIPE section. It is a "To Do" list for parents: take your child for wellness checkups, take your child on trips, offer your child opportunities to be with other children, listen to your child, tell stories and read with our child, and give your child plenty of opportunities to develop fine and gross motor skills by letting him play outside and cut, draw, or color inside.

I would like to conclude by including a "Do Not" list, or at least, a "Try Not to Do" list inspired by the work of Fisher in his book, *Teaching Children to Think* (1990). I cannot say that I have kept from doing all of these things; however, I am far better at giving than following my advice, especially when it comes to my own children. I still remember how I met my neighbor. Each week while our house was being built, we stopped by to see it in progress after Sunday school. With the children in their nice clothes, I reminded them to stay out of the mud piles. Unfortunately one Sunday, the mud piles were everywhere. When the children came back to the car after touring the property, not only wouldn't I let them get in, I screamed and hollered so loudly about me not having anything to wipe off their shoes that the neighbor ran outside with towels to help. It was an unsettling way to meet a new neighbor for the first time! Needless to say, I understand that it's sometimes hard for parents to take every piece of advice they've been given and implement it.

Fisher (1990) described both an encouraging and an inhibiting adult and how these types of adults work with children (see Table 10). The behaviors of the inhibiting adult remind us how easy it is to spoil our child's natural creativity and curiosity by being critical, judgmental, or disapproving. Although children have been shown to be resilient, it is in the parents' best interests to follow the guidelines of the encouraging adult instead.

Table 10
What Encouraging and Inhibiting Adults Do When Working With Children

Encouraging Adult	Inhibiting Adult
Actively listens	Is inattentive
Focuses on the child's thinking	Devalues the child's suggestions
Stresses independence	Promotes dependence
Treats the child as an equal	Acts as if he or she is superior to the child
Defers judgment	Is judgmental or critical
Sees learning in mistakes	Admonishes child for mistakes
Values creative ideas	Rejects new ideas
Optimistic about outcomes	Pessimistic about outcomes
Is sensitive, respectful, and nurturing	Is authoritative or disapproving

Note. Adapted from *Teaching Children to Think*, by R. Fisher, 1990, Oxford, England: Basil Blackwell.

Be interested in your child and his ideas, listen, and be positive and optimistic about your child's decisions. The ultimate goal in raising our children is for them to develop independence and lead happy and productive lives (without having to constantly consult their photographs of their mommy or pet in their pockets!).

My "Try Not to Do" list for parents of young children includes the following:

1. *Do not be unkind.* Although this sounds like a given, my heart broke recently when I overhead a woman in the grocery store

shouting to her toddler and her preschooler who were in the bottom of her grocery cart not to touch the food. She was putting the food on top of them—how could they not touch it?

2. *Do not be overprotective.* There are times when we simply must protect the safety of our children, but if they forget their gloves when they go outside, they will probably have cold hands and remember their gloves the next time. Decide when you can let natural consequences teach the lesson and when you need to intervene when safety *really* matters. Now that my youngest son is about to go off to college, he suggests that parents should be *influential*, but not overprotective.

3. *Do not push them to please you.* Ultimately, we want children doing things that please themselves, not their parents. Therefore, resist the temptation to say, "It will make me happy if you read with me." You want children to learn that reading with their parents can be fun and engaging for them, not you. Do not push children to read until they are ready— insisting that they "perform" when they read. Instead make reading an enjoyable family activity. This does not mean that children should never be taught to do things for others. What I am trying to say is not to connect students' academic accomplishments with the parents' feelings. They should be motivated to learn because it is exciting for them, not because they will please you.

4. *Do not praise intelligence. Praise effort.* Research by Dweck (2000) described two distinct theories people hold of intelligence: entity and incremental. When people hold an entity theory of intelligence, they believe that it is fixed and inherent. They think they should be able to do things without effort. Therefore, when tasks are challenging to them, they often feel defeated and will not try because they associate it

with their intelligence. If people hold an incremental theory of intelligence, they are more willing to try challenging tasks because they believe they can improve their intelligence with hard work and effort. Therefore, when something is difficult, they persist because they do not feel it is a lack of intelligence that is making it difficult, they feel that it may be a lack of strategy or effort. We need to give our children the incremental view of intelligence and praise them for hard work and effort.

5. *Do not lose your cool or behave like a child.* Be a positive role model. I once asked my two young sons to put their toys away. In a hurry they threw everything in the cabinet and did not pay attention to the way the toys were supposed to be sorted (animals, blocks, LEGOs, musical instruments, and so forth). I opened the cabinet and threw everything back out on the floor in a rage. They then quietly sorted and put all of the toys back, scared to death about my erratic behavior. It was my least proud moment of motherhood—and I still remember how bad I felt. They did not need to see me behave like a child. I should have conveyed my message matter-of-factly, and without emotion. They still would have had to redo the toy cabinet, but they would not have been worried about their mother. Whether we engage in good or bad behaviors, we are models for the behaviors that our children see. Let them see positive ones. While I pursued my doctoral degree, my children saw me study, read, and work hard. They, too, have learned the value of studying and working hard. I love to arrange flowers and bring candlelight to our dinner table. They, too, think about centerpieces and light candles for special meals. Our children are mindful of our behaviors, and we should be too.

Preparing your child for preschool is not just about academics. It's far more complex because we are preparing the *whole* child for a future life that includes spending less and less time with us. Building positive relationships with your child starts from the very beginning when they are putting their trust in you to feed and take care of their needs. You are responsible for both the physical and emotional environment surrounding your children because it influences them for the rest of their lives. When my oldest son left home for college, my questions were similar to the ones I asked when he went to kindergarten:

- Did I prepare him to get along with others?
- Did I show him how to become a kind, generous, and caring person?
- Did I prepare him to do things for himself and find resources if he needs them?
- Does he know that I love him and will be there to share his ups and downs?

Giving our children experiences that will help them later in life seems to be the easy part of our preparation. But, showing our children how we value their ideas, how we encourage their creative expression, and how we celebrate their accomplishments, not because they make us happy, but because they make them happy—that is what is important. My youngest son is now reading my favorite book, *The Little Prince* by Saint Exupéry. I am reminded again of the main message, "what is essential is invisible to the eye." The relationship you have between you and your child is the essential ingredient for both of you to be prepared not only for preschool but for lifelong learning. Enjoy your children. Indulge in creating fun and loving experiences together. Savor the precious moments of every stage of your child's life—we are always preparing for the next stage!

Resources
for Parents

THIS is the information age and everything we are wondering about is nearly a "finger click" away with the Internet. I have gathered in this section resources that relate to the topics of each chapter that I believe will be helpful when parents have questions about their children. I do not intend for it to be an exhaustive list, nor can I guarantee that by the time this book goes to print, these Web links will all work. The intention though is a good one, to start with something that will be useful to you, and to guide you on to the next click. I have included both general resources and a chapter-specific resource list.

General Resources

Books for Parents on Early Childhood

Bredekamp, S., & Rosegrant, T. (Eds.). (1995). *Reaching potentials: Transforming early childhood curriculum and assessment* (Vol. 2.). Washington, DC: National Association for the Education of Young Children.

Duckworth, E. (1996). *The having of wonderful ideas* (2nd ed.). New York: Teachers College Press.

Edwards, C., Gandini, L., & Forman, G. (1993). *The hundred languages of children: The Reggio Emilia approach to early childhood education*. Norwood, NJ: Ablex.

Ezzo, G., & Buckham, R. (2004). *On becoming preschool wise*. Sisters, OR: Parent Wise Solutions.

Feinburg, S., & Mindess, M. (1994). *Eliciting children's full potential: Designing and evaluating developmentally based programs for young children*. Pacific Grove, CA: Brooks/Cole Publishing.

Gonzalez-Mena, J. (2008). *Diversity in early care and education: Honoring differences* (5th ed.). New York: McGraw-Hill.

Helm, J. H., & Katz, L. (2001). *Young investigators*. New York: Teachers College Press.

Katz, L., & Chard, S. C. (2000). *Engaging children's minds: The project approach* (2nd ed.). Norwood, NJ: Ablex.

Kostelnik, M. J., Soderman, A. K., & Whiren, A. P. (1999). *Developmentally appropriate curriculum: Best practices in early childhood education* (2nd ed.). Upper Saddle River, NJ: Prentice-Hall.

McGillian, J. K. (2005). *The busy mom's book of preschool activities*. New York: Sterling.

Meier, D. (1995). *The power of their ideas*. Boston: Beacon Press.

Schulman, N., & Birnbaum, E. (2007). *Practical wisdom for parents: Demystifying the preschool years*. New York: Knopf.

Magazines for Parents and Young Children

Parents Magazine
http://www.parents.com

The Web site for *Parents* includes a special section on preschoolers, and the magazine often includes features specific to parents of preschoolers, as well. Some topics of interest include health and safety, socializing, and learning needs of this age group.

Child
http://www.child.com/common/magazine

Although this magazine separates itself from *Parents* by producing different issues with different topics, you'll find that most of the material online is the same. However, the magazine does include special topics of interest to parents of preschoolers.

FamilyFun
http://www.familyfun.go.com

Packed with activities for kids ranging from toddlers to age 12, this magazine features crafts, recipes, games, travel ideas, and holiday-themed activities for families to do together. The Web site includes a unique feature wherein parents can enter their child's age and current interest to find ideas specific to those interest areas.

Wondertime

http://www.wondertime.go.com

Wondertime, aimed at parents with children from infants to age 8, focuses on nurturing a child's love of learning. Its Web site includes activities to use at home, information on developing creative spaces, crafts and recipes, and links to blogs written by parents of young children.

Junior

http://www.juniormagazine.co.uk

Although this magazine is meant for parents in the UK, it is geared toward providing what it calls a "lively mix" of information, advice, and features about young children and babies. The Web site includes rotating features of special interest to parents.

Scholastic Parent and Child

http://www2.scholastic.com/browse/parentchild.jsp

This magazine aims to help parents keep pace with their chid's growth at home and school, focusing on intellectual, social, emotional, and physical development. Recent features have included using technology with kids and interviews with children's authors.

Nick Jr.

http://www.nickjr.com

Claiming it is the fasting growing magazine in the parenting category, *Nick Jr.* provides parents of kids ages birth to 11 with information about child development, home activities, child-related news and product reviews, and ideas for spending time as a family. Your child might enjoy playing the many interactive games on the Web site.

Highlights
http://www.highlights.com

Celebrating 60 years of existence, *Highlights* remains a popular favorite for kids and their parents. The magazine has undergone a redesign, but still includes traditional features such as Hidden Picture and Goofus and Gallant's good conduct information. The sister Web site, Highlights Kids (http://www.highlightskids.com) includes many activities of interest to the Web-savvy child.

Selected Journals for Parents on Early Childhood

Young Children
http://journal.naeyc.org

Young Children, published by the National Association for the Education of Young Children, is a bimonthly journal devoted to topical issues in early childhood education. Although the journal often covers educational practices, parents could get insight into their child's schooling by reading the articles included here.

Young Exceptional Children
http://yec.sagepub.com

Published by the Council for Exceptional Children's Division of Early Childhood, this journal is geared to teachers, families, and other caregivers of children with disabilities from birth to age 8. Each issue offers practical articles based on research and a list of comprehensive resources.

Parenting for High Potential
http://www.nagc.org/index.aspx?id=372

This quarterly journal, published by the National Association for Gifted Children, is designed for parents who want to help develop their children's gifts and talents. The Web site does include some of the back issues and sample articles online.

Chapter 1: Introduction

National Organizations With Resources for Parents

Council for Exceptional Children
http://www.cec.sped.org

The Council for Exceptional Children (CEC) is the largest international professional organization dedicated to improving educational outcomes for individuals with exceptionalities, students with disabilities, and/or the gifted. There are many resource materials for parents available through their Web site.

National Association for the Education of Young Children
http://www.naeyc.org

The National Association for the Education of Young Children (NAEYC) is dedicated to improving the well-being of all young children, with particular focus on the quality of educational and developmental services for all children from birth through age 8. The organization's Web site has a section for families in which parents can search for NAEYC accredited programs or download helpful information ranging from books for children to how parents can help young children cope after a disaster.

National Association for Gifted Children

http://www.nagc.org

The National Association for Gifted Children (NAGC) is an organization of parents, teachers, educators, other professionals, and community leaders who unite to address the unique needs of children and youth with demonstrated gifts and talents as well as those children who may be able to develop their talent potential with appropriate educational experiences. NAGC maintains an early childhood division of its organization and provides a special section on its Web site for parents.

National PTA

http://www.pta.org

The National Parent Teacher Association (PTA) remains the largest volunteer child advocacy association in the nation. Multiple resources for parent involvement and family-friendly discussions of educational policies and laws are included on the PTA site. Topics of help range from health and wellness, to media and technology, to safety, to discussions of No Child Left Behind. The PTA also produces a magazine for parents and families.

National Autism Association

http://www.nationalautismassociation.org

This organization provides information to families and teachers about autism, has links to support groups, research, and events that help families of children with autism.

Helpful Web sites

Getting Ready: School Readiness Indicators Initiative
http://www.gettingready.org/matriarch

This helpful site provides kids' facts, information on various indicators of school readiness, links to Web resources, and articles and reports on the Initiative's findings.

University of Michigan Health System,
Developmental Milestones
http://www.med.umich.edu/1libr/yourchild/devmile.htm

This Web site provides a nice overview of typical childhood development and includes links to lists of developmental milestones for children from ages 1 month to 5 years, under overall development, social and emotional development, and speech and language development.

Tufts University Child and Family WebGuide
http://www.cfw.tufts.edu

The Child and Family WebGuide is a unique resource for parents of young children, because it provides a directory of Web sites evaluated and critiqued by experts in early childhood education at Tufts University. Parents can choose to either select resources by topic, by age group, or by an A–Z listing. Each Web site listing also includes a starred rating to see how it performed to the Tufts University standards.

Chapter 2: What Can Parents Do?

Helpful Web Sites

The Illinois Early Learning Project Tip Sheets
http://illinoisearlylearning.org/tipsheets/homeactivities.htm

This site provides many tips for helping turn home activities into learning activities. The tip sheets are accessible in both English and Spanish.

Activities to Help Your Child Learn About Language
http://www.ed.gov/Family/GrowthChart/page2.html

This site provides a breakdown of activities that build language and literacy development in children from birth to age 6 years.

Let's Write!
http://www.ed.gov/pubs/parents/LearnPtnrs/write.html

Discussing what parents can do to show the importance of writing skills with young children, this site includes several kid-friendly activities parents can incorporate easily into their everyday experiences, based on research done by the National Center for the Study of Writing and Literacy.

Helping Your Preschool Child
http://www.ed.gov/parents/earlychild/ready/preschool/part.html

This site is home to the mini-book by the same name, published by the U.S. Department of Education. Parents can access the book in English and Spanish by downloading a pdf copy or calling the contact information on the Web page to request a copy.

PBS Parents Guide to Children and Media
http://www.pbs.org/parents/childrenandmedia/article-faq.
html

This Web site has links to age-appropriate checklists for uses of television, computers, video games, and movies. It also discusses the prevalence of TV watching in young children, while offering alternatives and suggestions for parent monitoring of media time, along with results of research studies conducted on the effects of TV viewing at a young age.

Scholastic Parents
http://www2.scholastic.com/browse/parentsHome.jsp

Scholastic provides a comprehensive site for parents with a parent newsletter and online help in four main topics: School & Learning, Activities, Books & Reading, and Family Life. Recently, the site included two features of interest to parents of preschoolers, one on preschoolers' learning styles and one on books for early readers.

The following Web sites are great for parents and kids to explore together.

U.S. Department of Agriculture Food Pyramid for Kids
http://www.mypyramid.gov/kids

This site provides colorful copies of the recently revised Food Pyramid for Kids, including posters with information on the various food groups and tips for healthy living. Coloring pages and an interactive game also help promote healthy eating for children.

Children's Museum of Indianapolis
http://www.childrensmuseum.org

In addition to giving information related to current exhibits, there is a section on the Web site for children in grades PreK–2 to play games that engage your child in creative thinking.

Cool Science for Curious Kids
http://www.hhmi.org/coolscience

Sponsored by the Howard Hughes Medical Institute, this Web site invites young children to explore biology. By asking an engaging question, students are motivated to find out more about plants, butterflies, animals, and microorganisms. They even learn that they can make a salad with all of the parts of a plant.

Fun Sites for Preschoolers
http://www.tempe.gov/youthlibrary/preschool/preschweb.htm

This site includes a long list of a variety of Web sites parents can explore with their preschoolers.

Creativity: Nurture and Protect Your Child's Creative Spirit
http://www.pbs.org/parents/creativity

Included are creativity-based games—drawing, plumbing, and making shadows, among others—for parents to play with their children. The site also provides examples for parents to inspire them to create homes where creativity flourishes.

Children's Authors and Publishers Web Pages

Many favorite children's authors now have Web sites where children may interact with the stories, see short video clips, contact the author, or purchase books and other paraphernalia that goes with the stories.

Stan and Jan Berenstain (Berenstain Bears books)
http://www.berenstainbears.com

This Web site includes activities parents can do with their children and short video clips of stories. Activities include trivia quizzes, coloring pages, puzzles, facts about animals, and an interactive storybook.

Jan Brett
http://www.janbrett.com

This Web site is filled with activities (listed from A–Z) that parents can do with their children that relate to Jan Brett stories. A wide range of activities are included, with instructions for everything from puppet making, to flash cards, to math facts, to drawing tips, to creating holiday placemats. Kids might like sending e-mail postcards to friends and family or creating their own cards through this site.

Shel Silverstein
http://www.shelsilverstein.com

His Web site includes downloadable color and activity books that engage children in creating and reading their own poetry. There are puzzles, games, a poetry kit, and a downloadable activity booklet, all featuring Silverstein's artwork and poetry.

I Spy Books

http://www.scholastic.com/ispy

This Web site has activities for children and information for parents and teachers. Kids can play their favorite I Spy games with rotating puzzle pages. With adult help, children also can make their own I SPY riddles and pictures.

Chapter 3: Enhancing Social and Emotional Competencies

Center on the Social and Emotional Foundations
for Early Learning
http://www.vanderbilt.edu/csefel

The center is located at Vanderbilt University under the direction of Professor Mary Louise Hemmeter. The purpose of their center is to develop materials that reflect evidence-based practices for promoting children's social and emotional development and preventing challenging behaviors. This site has downloadable activities to do with children's books that teach children about emotions.

CSEFEL Practical Strategies
http://www.vanderbilt.edu/csefel/practicalstrategies.html

This site has a wealth of links and downloadable materials for parents. PDF booklets designed to teach social and emotional skills and tools for working on building relationships are provided. The Book Nook has modules for each of the selected books that give various activities parents or teachers could do that match selected concepts covered in the book. In addition, the center has scripted social stories for parents or teachers to use in teaching social and emotional skills.

Chapter 4: Choosing a Preschool

NAEYC will provide a complimentary brochure entitled, "A Good Preschool for Your Child" if you send a self-addressed, stamped, business size envelope to the following address: NAEYC, Box 517, 1509 16th Street, N.W., Washington, DC 20036.

Helpful Web Sites

Project Approach Curriculum
http://www.ed.uiuc.edu/ups/projects

Visit the University Primary School at the University of Illinois Urbana-Champaign Web site to see examples of young students engaged in project investigations. There are two preschool investigations—one entitled "Exploring Fire Safety," and the other called "Studying Music." Each project investigation is organized according to the phases of project work. Digital photo galleries and videos are available for some projects. You will see how the activities in the project investigation relate to learning standards across the various disciplines. In addition to seeing children engaged in projects, you also may view information about the Project Approach and links to other resources on project-based learning.

North Central Regional Educational Laboratory (NCREL)
http://www.ncrel.org

This Web site includes links to research on school readiness, early childhood environments, key concepts on early childhood practices, as well as links to information about Montessori and Reggio Emilia inspired preschools and the Project Approach.

Reggio Inspired
http://www.reggioinspired.com

Although this site was created with Singapore in mind, much of the information about the Reggio Emilia approach will be useful to parents considering schools that adopt this approach (or adopt particular pieces of this approach). It also includes recommended readings and useful links for parents.

The International Montessori Index
http://www.montessori.edu

This site provides a good bit of information on Montessori schooling, including advice for parents wanting to find a strictly Montessori school. It also includes advice for using the Montessori method with children ages birth to 12.

The Montessori Foundation,
The International Montessori Council
http://www.montessori.org

This Web site, the site of the International Montessori Council, also provides help for parents wanting to find a Montessori school, along with online articles about parenting "the Montessori way," and information on the several magazines and journals the organization publishes in support of Montessori education.

Association of Waldorf Schools of North America
http://www.awsna.org/awsna.html

The Web site describes Waldorf education and has links to purchase materials, to join newsletters, and to see special events.

Preschool and Kindergarten in the Waldorf Schools
http://www.whywaldorfworks.org/02_W_Education/pre_
and_k.asp

This Web site describes how Waldorf education is implemented for preschool and kindergarten children. From this site, parents can access myriad information on Waldorf education, including frequently asked questions and resources.

National Head Start Association
http://www.nhsa.org

The NHSA represents the needs of the more than 1 million children and their families, teachers, and communities. Advocating for policies that affect Head Start programs, the organization includes articles on recent legislation on its Web site. Other items of interest may include information on advocacy campaigns and programs and an online magazine for families.

Chapter 5: Strengthening Partnerships Between School and Home

Helpful Web Site

National Coalition for Parent Involvement in Education
http://www.ncpie.org

The mission of the National Coalition for Parent Involvement in Education (NCPIE) is to advocate the involvement of parents and families in their children's education, and to foster relationships between home, school, and community to enhance the education of all our nation's young people. On the Web site is an abundant set of resources for parents, educators, and community members to support building a better learning community for young children. More than 180 listings of books, articles, and curricular materials that relate to building partnerships with families and schools are included. In addition, the site links parents to other organizations that have similar missions and goals. Most states also provide Web sites that show best practice in developing healthy partnerships between schools and families.

Chapter 6: Letting Go: Making the Transition From Home to School

Helpful Web Site

Terrific Transitions: Supporting Children's Transitions to Kindergarten
http://www.serve.org/TT/transiti.html

This Web site has many resources for parents and families that relate to transitions. Specifically, there are tip sheets, booklets that can be downloaded, and additional resources for parents. Although many of the materials are specifically related to transitions from preschool to kindergarten, the tips for parents are appropriate for all early childhood transitions. All of the materials are translated into Spanish. Also there are calendars for each month with activities for parents and children to do together.

Books for Children About School and the Transition to School

Berenstain Bears Go to School by Stan and Jan Berenstain
Clifford's First School Day by Norman Bridwell
What to Expect at Preschool by Heidi Eisenburg Murkoff
D.W.'s Guide to Preschool by Marc Brown
My First Day at Nursery School by Becky Edwards
I Love You All Day Long by Francesca Rusackas
Mouse's First Day of School by Lauren Thompson
Don't Go! by Jane Breskin Zalben
Will You Come Back for Me? by Ann Tompert

References

Associated Press. (2004). *Report: Obesity rising sharply among U.S. preschoolers.* Retrieved March 20, 2008, from http://www.cnn.com/2004/HEALTH/conditions/12/30/childhood.obesity/index.html

Association of Waldorf Schools of North America. (n.d.). *Waldorf education: Frequently asked questions.* Retrieved March 25, 2008, from http://www.whywaldorfworks.org/02_W_Education/faq_about.asp

Ayres, K. (2005, October 3). Bilingual preschool programs expand. *Dallas Morning News.* Retrieved March 24, 2008, from http://www.latinamericanstudies.org/latinos/preschool.htm

Ayres, K. (2007, August 17). A new translation. *Dallas Morning News.* Retrieved March 24, 2008, from http://www.dallasnews.com/sharedcontent/dws/news/localnews/stories/DN-dualanguage_17met.ART.North.Edition1.4232880.html

Blain, D., & Deal, L. K. (1991). *The Boxcar Children cookbook.* Morton Grove, IL: Albert Whitman.

Blaydes, J. (2003). *The educator's book of quotes.* Thousand Oaks, CA: Corwin Press.

Brennan, G. (2006). *Green eggs & ham cookbook.* New York: Random House.

Centers for Disease Control and Prevention. (2007). *Autism spectrum disorders overview.* Retrieved March 20, 2008, from http://www.cdc.gov/ncbddd/autism/overview.htm

Center on the Social and Emotional Foundations for Early Learning (CSEFEL). (2007). *Positive solutions for families* [DVD]. Urbana-Champaign: University of Illinois at Urbana-Champaign.

The Century Foundation. (2000). *Universal preschool.* Retrieved March 24, 2008, from http://www.tcf.org/Publications/Education/UniversalPreschool.pdf

Children's Defense Fund. (2005). *Head Start basics.* Retrieved March 24, 2008, from http://www.childrensdefense.org/site/DocServer/headstartbasics2005.pdf?docid=616

Dahl, R., & Dahl, F. (1997). *Roald Dahl's revolting recipes.* New York: Puffin.

Dahl, R., & Dahl, F. (2003). *Roald Dahl's even more revolting recipes.* New York: Puffin.

Demers, P. (2003). *From instruction to delight: An anthology of children's literature to 1850.* New York: Oxford University Press.

Dreikurs, R., & Goldman, M. (1990). *The ABCs of guiding the child.* Chicago: Adler School

Dweck, C. (2000). *Self-theories. Their role in motivation, personality, and development.* Philadelphia: Psychology Press.

Edwards, C., Gandini, L., & Forman, G. (1993). *The hundred languages of children: The Reggio Emilia approach to early childhood education.* Norwood, NJ: Ablex.

Epstein, A. S. (2007). *The intentional teacher: Choosing the best strategies for young children's learning.* Washington, DC: National Association for the Education of Young Children.

Feinburg, S., & Mindess, M. (1994). *Eliciting children's full potential: Designing and evaluating developmentally based programs for young children.* Pacific Grove, CA: Brooks/Cole Publishing.

Fisher, R. (1990). *Teaching children to think.* Oxford, England: Basil Blackwell Ltd.

Fulghum, R. (1989). *All I really need to know I learned in kindergarten.* New York: Ballantine Books.

Gartrell, D. (2004). *The power of guidance: Teaching social-emotional skills in early childhood classrooms.* Cliffton Park, NY: Delmar Learning.

Goals 2000 Educate America Act, Pub. Law 103-227 (March 31, 1994).

Gold, R. (2006). *Kids cook 1-2-3.* New York: Bloomsbury USA.

Helm, J., Beneke, S., & Steinheimer, K. (2007). *Windows on learning* (2nd ed.). New York: Teachers College Press.

Hennessey, B. A. (2005). Developing creativity in gifted children: The central importance of motivation and classroom climate. NAGC Newsletter. Storrs, CT: National Research Center on the Gifted and Talented.

Heroman, C. (2005). *The creative curriculum study starters.* Washington, DC: Teaching Strategies.

Illinois Early Learning Project. (2007). *Fun at home with preschoolers: Getting ready to read!* Retrieved March 15, 2008, from http://illinoisearlylearning.org/tipsheets/homeactivities.htm

Illinois State Board of Education. (2008). *Preschool for all.* Retrieved March 19, 2008, from http://www.isbe.net/earlychi/preschool/default.htm

Individuals with Disabilities Education Improvement Act, PL 108-446, 118 Stat. 2647 (2004).

International Reading Association. (1997). *Exploring the playground of books: Tips for parents of beginning readers.* Retrieved April 14, 2008, from http://www.reading.org/downloads/parents/pb1019_playground.pdf

Jablon, J., & Stetson, C. (2007). Tips for talking with children. *Teaching Young Children, 1,* 8–9.

Kang, J. (2007). How many languages can Reggio children speak? Many more than a hundred! *Gifted Child Today, 30*(3), 45–48, 65.

Kantrowitz, B., & Wingert, P. (1991, December 2). The 10 best schools in the world. *Newsweek, 18*(23), 50. Retrieved March 25, 2008, from http://www.reggioinspired.com/newsweek.htm

Katz, L. (1995). *Talks with teachers of young children: A collection.* Norwood, NJ: Ablex.

Katz, L. (2007). What to look for when visiting early childhood classes. *Gifted Child Today, 30*(3), 34–37.

Katz, L. G., & Chard, S. C. (2000). *Engaging children's minds: The project approach* (2nd ed.). Norwood, NJ: Ablex.

McClellan, D., & Katz, L. G. (2001). *Assessing young children's social competence.* Champaign, IL: ERIC Clearinghouse on Elementary and Early Childhood Education. (ERIC Document Reproduction Service No. ED356100). Retrieved March 24, 2008, from http://ceep.crc.uiuc.edu/eecearchive/digests/2001/mcclel01.pdf

MacGregor, C. (1980). *The storybook cookbook*. Upper Saddle River, NJ: Prentice-Hall.

Moore, S. (2000). *The fairy tale cookbook*. Nashville, TN: Cumberland House.

National Association for the Education of Young Children. (1998). Learning to read and write: Developmentally appropriate practices for young children. A joint position statement of the International Reading association and the National Association for the Education of Young Children. *Young Children, 53*(4), 30–46.

National Association for the Education of Young Children. (2004). *Where we stand on school readiness*. Washington, DC: Author. Retrieved March 19, 2008, from http://www.naeyc.org/about/positions/pdf/Readiness.pdf

National Association for the Education of Young Children. (n.d.a). *Technology and young children: Ages 3 through 8*. Retrieved March 24, 2008, from http://www.naeyc.org/about/positions/PSTECH98.asp

National Association for the Education of Young Children. (n.d.b). *NAEYC Early childhood program standards*. Retrieved March 24, 2008, from http://www.naeyc.org/academy/standards

National Association for the Education of Young Children. (n.d.c). *Standard 2: NAEYC accreditation criteria for curriculum*. Retrieved December 29, 2007, from http://www.naeyc.org/academy/standards/standard2/standard2A.asp

National Association of State Boards of Education. (1991). *Caring communities: Supporting young children and families. The report of the National Task Force on School Readiness* (Report No. PS020642). Alexandria, VA: Author. (ERIC Document Reproduction Service No. ED358908)

National Institute of Mental Health. (2008). *Autism spectrum disorders (Pervasive developmental disorders).* Retrieved March 20, 2008, from http://www.nimh.nih.gov/health/publications/autism/complete-publication.shtml

National School Readiness Indicators Initiative. (2005). *Getting ready: Executive summary.* Providence: Rhode Island KIDS COUNT. Retrieved March 19, 2008, from http://www.gettingready.org/matriarch/d.asp?PageID=303&PageNam e2=pdfhold&p=PageName=Getting+Ready+%2D+Executiv e+Summary%2Epdf

No Child Left Behind Act, 20 U.S.C. §6301 (2001).

Patten, P., & Ricks, O. M. (2000). *Child care quality: An overview for parents.* Champaign, IL: ERIC Clearinghouse on Elementary and Early Childhood Education. (ERIC Digest No. EDO-PS-00-14)

PBS Parents. (2008a). *Children and media: TV and kids under age 3.* Retrieved March 14, 2008, from http://www.pbs.org/parents/childrenandmedia/article-faq.html

PBS Parents. (2008b). *Children and media: Computers: Preschoolers.* Retrieved March 14, 2008, from http://www.pbs.org/parents/childrenandmedia/computers-preschool.html

Peterson, N. (2006). *Encouraging your child's writing talent: The involved parents' guide.* Waco, TX: Prufrock Press.

Preschool for All. (n.d.). *About Preschool for All.* Retrieved March 20, 2008, from http://www.preschoolforall.org/aboutus.htm

Ready at Five. (2004). *What works? Promising practices for improving the school readiness of English language learners.* Baltimore: Author. Retrieved March 24, 2008, from http://www.readyatfive.org/images/pdfs/whatworks.pdf

Riley, D., San Juan, R. R., Klinkner, J., & Ramminger, A. (2008). *Social & emotional development*. St. Paul, MN: Redleaf Press.

Reggio Children, & Project Zero (2001). *Making learning visible. Children as individual and group learners*. Reggio Emilia, Italy: Reggio Children.

Rosenbaum, S. (2006). *Williams-Sonoma kids in the kitchen: Fun food*. New York: Free Press.

Silverman, S. M., & Weinfeld, R. (2007). *School success for kids with Asperger's syndrome*. Waco, TX: Prufrock Press.

Tabors, P. O., & López, L. M. (2005). *How can teachers and parents help young children become (and stay) bilingual?* Retrieved March 24, 2008, from http://www.headstartinfo.org/publications/hsbulletin78/hsb78_10fix.htm

Travers, P. L. (2006). *Mary Poppins in the kitchen*. New York: Harcourt.

Tyre, P. (2006, September 11). The new first grade: Too much too soon. *Newsweek*. Retrieved March 19, 2008, from http://www.newsweek.com/id/45571

U.S. Census Bureau. (2002). *Who's minding the kids? Child care arrangements: Winter 2002*. Retrieved March 21, 2008, from http://www.census.gov/prod/2005pubs/p70-101.pdf

U.S. Department of Agriculture. (n.d.) *Tips for families*. Retrieved January 31, 2008, from http://teamnutrition.usda.gov/resources/mpk_tips.pdf

U.S. Department of Health and Human Services. (2005a). *Head Start regulations*, 45 CFR 1305.6(c). Washington, DC: Author. Retrieved March 24, 2008, from http://www.acf.hhs.gov/programs/hsb/pdf/1305_ALL.pdf

U.S. Department of Health and Human Services. (2005b). *Supporting English language learners through family literacy services*. Retrieved March 24, 2008, from http://www.

headstartinfo.org/publications/hsbulletin78/hsb78_09. htm

Unger, M. (2001). Equalizing the status of both languages in a dual immersion school. *The ACIE Newsletter, 5*(1). Retrieved March 24, 2008, from http://www. carla.umn.edu/ immersion/acie/vol5/Nov2001_EqualStatus.html

United Way of America. (2008). *Early childhood success by 6*. Retrieved March 19, 2008, from http://www.unitedway. org/sb6

United Way of Champaign County. (2006–2007). *Success by 6 kindergarten readiness checklist*. Champaign, IL: Author.

Vygotsky, L. S. (1978). *Mind and society: The development of higher psychological processes*. Cambridge, MA: Harvard University Press.

Walker, B. (1989). *The Little House cookbook*. New York: HarperTrophy.

Weinfeld, R., & Davis, M. (2008). *Special needs advocacy resource book*. Waco, TX: Prufrock Press.

Westfield Community School. (2007). *Readiness skills*. Retrieved July 10, 2007, from http://www.d300.org/web/schoolsites/ westfieldcommunityschool/elementarypages/kindergarten/ readinessskills.html

About the Author

NANCY B. HERTZOG, PH.D., is associate professor in the Department of Special Education at the University of Illinois at Urbana-Champaign. Hertzog has an extensive background in gifted education and expertise on curriculum development. She directs University Primary School, an early childhood gifted education program with a diverse multicultural staff and student population. Her research focuses on curricular approaches and teaching strategies designed to differentiate instruction and challenge children with diverse abilities.

Specifically, she has studied teachers' implementation of the Project Approach in classrooms with both high-achieving and low-achieving children. Hertzog has written Web-based curricular guides that detail project investigations of preschool, kindergarten, and first-grade students that have won national recognition from the National Association for Gifted Children.

Hertzog has served as the chair of the Early Childhood Division of the National Association for Gifted Children and previously served as co-chair of the Education Commission of the National Association for Gifted Children. She also sits on the Board of Directors for the Illinois Association for Gifted Children and the Editorial Board of *Roeper Review*.

She has published in the *Journal of Curriculum Studies, Gifted Child Quarterly, Journal for the Education of the Gifted, Roeper Review, Teaching Exceptional Children, Early Childhood Research and Practice*, and *Young Exceptional Children*. Hertzog has received grants to integrate technology into early childhood settings and train classroom teachers to use digital photography for assessment and documentation of student growth.

CPSIA information can be obtained at www.ICGtesting.com
Printed in the USA
BVOW031748240212

283758BV00005B/147/P